DIVERSITY AND CITIZENSHIP

DIVERSITY AND CITIZENSHIP

Rediscovering American Nationhood

Gary Jeffrey Jacobsohn
and
Susan Dunn

ROWMAN & LITTLEFIELD PUBLISHERS, INC.

ROWMAN & LITTLEFIELD PUBLISHERS, INC.

Published in the United States of America
by Rowman & Littlefield Publishers, Inc.
4720 Boston Way, Lanham, Maryland 20706

3 Henrietta Street
London WC2E 8LU, England

British Cataloging in Publication Information Available

Library of Congress Cataloging-in-Publication Data

Diversity and citizenship : rediscovering American nationhood /
[edited] by Gary Jeffrey Jacobsohn and Susan Dunn.
p. cm.
Lectures presented as part of the celebration of the bicentennial of the founding of
Williams College.
Includes bibliographical references and index.
1. Citizenship—United States. 2. Civil society—United States.
3. Individualism—United States. 4. Multiculturalism—United States. 5. Pluralism
(Social sciences)—United States.
I. Jacobsohn, Gary J. II. Dunn, Susan. III. Williams College.
JK1763.D59 1995 306.2'0973—dc20 95-23771 CIP

ISBN 0-8476-8091-6 (cloth : alk. paper)
ISBN 0-8476-8092-4 (pbk. : alk. paper)

Printed in the United States of America

♾™ The paper used in this publication meets the minimum requirements of
American National Standard for Information Sciences—Permanence of
Paper for Printed Library Materials, ANSI Z39.48–1984.

Contents

Acknowledgments

The essays in this book were originally presented as lectures in 1993 as part of the celebrations for the bicentennial of the founding of Williams College, Williamstown, Massachusetts. We wish to thank the director of the Francis C. Oakley Center for the Humanities and Social Sciences at Williams, Jean-Bernard Bucky, for helping to sponsor these lectures on Diversity and Citizenship. Thanks are also due to Shirley Bushika, Donna Chenail, Becky Brassard, and Peggy Bryant in the Faculty Secretarial Office for their help in preparing this manuscript.

Introduction

by Gary Jeffrey Jacobsohn and Susan Dunn

The post-Cold War world order has become a spawning ground for new polities. Designing constitutions for these regimes, we are learning, is almost as challenging a task as creating guidelines and rules for the achievement of orderly relations in a dramatically changed international environment. Common to both of these projects is a vexing set of problems associated with the passions and conflicts of multiple nationalisms. Only with their resolution can the prospect of a just and stable political future become a realistic possibility.

While established polities such as the United States have been only witnesses to the extraordinary societal upheavals of recent years, the political currents that have transformed much of the world have, in more muted form, also stimulated important reassessments of some basic questions of political and constitutional meaning within the spectator states. Of these, perhaps the most intriguing one concerns the nature, status, and implications of membership in the political community. The heightened attention in recent years to ascriptive loyalties and their claims upon the state has provided a fresh context for examining the obligations and character of contemporary citizenship.

This examination is occurring at all levels of society and government, from local school boards to bar associations, to state and federal courtrooms, to congressional committees. The essays in this volume highlight the surge of interest in the investigation of these matters within academic circles. The scholars represented here are all concerned with the connection between citizenship and nationhood, between individual and collective identities. This is not to presume that there is in fact such a relationship; after all, an old and quite popular view has it that in the modern liberal state (exemplified by the United States) the phenomenon of individual identity exists in splendid isolation from whatever collective meaning is discoverable in the nation or larger body politic. Thus in this view citizenship is a purely legalistic designation, carrying minimal (if any) significance for what it might reveal about the nation as a whole. It is also quite minimalist in what it requires of the citizen, whose efforts to go it alone in establishing an individual identity tend to leave precious little time for the advancement of the public good.

There has always been an important strand in the liberal political tradition that has resisted the idea that membership in the political community requires the subordination of one's own interests to those of others. Often this strand manifests itself in an emphasis on conscience as an individual good that must be accommodated by law and policy. A radical extension of this individualistic claim sometimes leads to an expectation of law's subordination to conscience, but this ultimately calls into question the very same liberal assumptions that nourish individualism. Thus arguably bound up in the idea of American citizenship is the bedrock and regime-defining principle of natural equality, according to which claims grounded in the superior obligation of conscience are not entitled to special consideration. As John Locke maintained, ''[T]he private judgment of any Person concerning a Law . . . does not take away the Obligation of that Law.''

But there is also a very different expression of this radical individualism, depicted jurisprudentially in Oliver Wendell Holmes's classic formulation of the ''bad man'' theory of the law, a philosophical stance that makes a virtue out of egotistical self-interest maximization. In his essay, Robert Dahl is unwilling to accept the consequences of the Holmesian model, which he would characterize as an unacceptable concession to ''hyperegoism.'' Implicit in contemporary rational choice models is a culture of political cynicism that is both morally repulsive and contrary to our founding ideals as a nation. On the other hand, Dahl dismisses the possibility of a politics of civic virtue—classical republicanism's commitment to a public good that presumes significant individual sacrifice. Such a solution is simply incompatible with a society as economically and culturally diverse as exists in the United States. ''Heroic altruism,'' he argues, is rarely possible in a large heterogeneous polity. Instead he proposes a middle position, which he calls the ''politics of robust civility,'' emphasizing a heightened attention to process as a way of encouraging fairness and enlightened understanding.

Sanford Levinson, on the other hand, lacks confidence in the American political culture's capacity to sustain an elevated view of citizenship, and he is consequently reluctant to reject the Holmesian model. Focusing specifically on the practice of law, Levinson explores the tension between citizenship and professionalism. His analysis of this relationship leads him to reflect on an alternative political and legal culture—Latvia. This encounter with one of the newly independent Soviet republics suggests some of the tradeoffs in these two opposing notions of a lawyer's responsibilities to the polity and common good. Levinson examines, for example, how, in particular political contexts, the role of national citizenship in structuring our identities cannot and ought not be underplayed. Thus in Latvia, a small country with poignant and historic reasons for wishing to maintain a strong sense of national identity, the profession of lawyering is linked to an engaged citizenry that may, unlike in the United States, require attorneys to counsel their clients in a manner that places the common good above individual aggrandizement. If, as a polity, we are a "state of many nations," then, Levinson suggests, perhaps our egoism is not entirely misplaced, but we should resist efforts to establish our experience as a model for indiscriminate emulation.

Whatever side one takes in the dispute between liberals and republicans on the benefits and liabilities of a "thin" conception of citizenship, it is nevertheless true that the American model of nationhood, in which a set of principles becomes the very soul of the nation, establishes certain parameters around the concept of citizenship. In the current debate over multiculturalism, it has been contended against both those who define the nation as little more than a collection of groups and those who define it as the realization of an idea, that a cultural conception of nationhood, emphasizing the historic connections of the American people to a particular religious or ethnic tradition, presents the best account of who Americans are as a nation. But, to the extent that this notion leads to depriving people of their full rights of citizenship solely on the basis of primordial attachments such as race, religion, or ethnicity, then such a definition is clearly incompatible with the logic of a nation defined by its dedication to certain "self-evident" principles of political morality. Conversely, the privileging of any group based on such attachments, by conferring upon its members extra citizenship benefits and rewards, would be similarly suspect. The fundamental proposition here is that full and equal membership in the political community is not to be affected by one's contingent affiliation, that a particular identity shall not be permitted to encroach upon the constitutive domain of political identity.

Pauline Maier's essay on the political significance of the American Revolution reminds us that in our early days this logic was not always followed, even if citizenship was extraordinarily comprehensive, for its day, in the range of its inclusiveness. But in emphasizing the political nature of the Revolution, namely, the decisive fact that the American nation was born of a revolution that was premised on assumptions about the popular origins of all legitimate authority, she shows how the character of the nation and its citizens are closely bound in an important way. Thus in her examination of eloquent provincial and local documents outlining the reasons for independence, she finds significance in these appeals for their having cut across profound political and social differences, establishing, as it were, a source of a shared and common identity. One is reminded here of Abraham Lincoln's famous reference to "our fathers [who] brought forth a new nation, conceived in Liberty, and dedicated to the proposition that all men are created equal." In the context of their delivery, these thoughts were meant to indicate that our future as a nation was inseparable from its creation, or, in other words, that it was uniquely dependent upon the affirmation and progressive realization of the revolutionary principles that gave original definition to the nation.

Those revolutionary principles have been the subject of continuing scholarly debate. One aspect of that debate has its roots in the early contest between Federalists and Anti-Federalists over the role of a constitution in the development of a common American identity. In Noah Pickus's subtle reevaluation of these arguments, we see how Dahl's call for a "politics of robust civility" echoes the appeals of the Federalists for a constitutional arrangement that would establish the basis for a common sense of peoplehood without foreclosing subsequent deliberation over the nature of our common identity. Thus the Constitution is not seen as an instrument of a people already formed by the sentiments expressed in the documents studied in Maier's account, but rather is itself instrumental in creating that people. According to Pickus, it was the Anti-Federalists who insisted that the Constitution lock in a predetermined national creed; that, for example, their arguments for inclusion of a Bill of Rights represented an important commitment to limiting the scope of subsequent deliberations over the principles that would define our common identity. If Pickus's reading of Publius's intentions is correct, then in a period of heightened multicultural awareness, his argument has considerable potential for addressing some of the challenges faced by advocates of a political culture grounded in shared values.

Indeed, in the United States at the end of the twentieth century, many of the principles of our "common culture" are being reevaluated. Under siege, for example, is the traditional notion of "e pluribus unum," as when different groups insist that they do not wish to be incorporated into an homogeneous American "unum." While the related concept of a common good, also entailing the creation of one out of many, has always been an elusive goal, it is vehemently denounced by many today as a false goal, as lacking legitimacy on it own terms. Whether the universalism that is the great legacy of the Enlightenment is derided as a mask for Eurocentrism and colonialism or simply seen as a naive objective of a failed liberalism, its very survival as a legacy of eighteenth-century political and scientific thought is seriously in question.

In this regard, Nathan Glazer reminds us of an earlier time when assimilation was largely taken for granted, when a principal goal of public education was Americanization. One need only recall the traditional school pageant of a few decades ago: students, dressed as immigrants, each wearing the distinctive costume of a different nation, enter a giant cardboard melting pot at the center of the school stage. From the other side of the melting pot, the students emerge, all dressed alike. This theatre of assimilation was emblematic of an age when commitment to the principles of the Constitution, including a willingness to deemphasize national, ethnic, and religious differences, was supposed to denote the essence of citizenship. But this has increasingly become a difficult position to sustain, and Glazer understandably wonders whether there is a viable alternative in today's vastly different cultural scene.

Today, he points out, the "triumphalist view of the history of American inclusion" lacks the legitimacy that was once a part of its universal scholarly acceptance. An alternative account of what constitutes the "mainstream" of American history emphasizes racism, chauvinism, and exclusion. Although Glazer makes clear that his own views on this subject are closer to the older account, he acknowledges the strength of the other side. Along the way, he notes that the faith in progressive inclusion of all groups in the American nation that framed his critique of affirmative action twenty years ago can no longer be stated with the boldness and self-confidence that accompanied its original assertion. It is in this context that he explores two central paradoxes of American citizenship, one of which bears directly on the coexistence of formal equality with a pervasive mindset that would deny the fullness of membership in the American nation to groups of people on the basis of race and nationality. Focusing our attention on one of the important battlefields where different and opposing concepts of citizenship are clashing—the social studies curriculum—Glazer reveals just how complex are the issues surrounding the contemporary debate over multiculturalism. Underlying all of his concerns is the matter of whether the schools are capable of playing a role in the teaching and formation of citizenship and civic virtue.

Glazer's reflections are particularly applicable to the question that has effectively established parameters for debate over the character of American citizenship: the status of African-Americans within the political community. Randall Kennedy shows how the historical facts surrounding the much contested issue of African Americans' inclusion as citizens of the republic have been distorted and manipulated in the service of political ends. Moreover, these inaccuracies are not limited to only one point on the political spectrum, but rather, as Kennedy's discussion of the unlikely pairing of Roger Taney and Thurgood Marshall suggests, inaccuracies have served radically different agendas. Thus, in the accounts of both Taney and Marshall—the latter appropriating the earlier justice's dubious history concerning the Framers' intentions for the free black population—we see how both oppressor and oppressed have used constitutional silences and ambiguities to address contemporary needs.

The significance of this controversy extends well beyond the relatively narrow interests of the followers of academic or legal disputation. Indeed it goes to the core of the American conception of nationhood. For if Taney was correct in his denial that people of African descent were, *or could ever be*, citizens of the United States, that the unalienable natural rights affirmed in the Declaration of Independence as the common possession of all men had never been intended to apply to them, then the character of this nation would be very different from what many have believed it is. Thus Martin Luther King, Jr.'s famous reference in 1963 to the Declaration as a "promissory note" echoes Lincoln's sentiments about the aspirational quality of American founding principles. Their intent is clear. The principles are to disabuse us of any exclusionary inference that might be drawn from the failure of the polity to deliver equal rights to all its constituent groups. As Kennedy makes clear, this is the view also held by Frederick Douglass, who once asked the question that suggests the dilemma of all peoples who have not experienced full membership in the American political community: "What country have I?" His eventual answer could not be reconciled with Taney's history, for it presumed that the identification of the nation with a set of ideals rather than with a flawed and unjust past, carried with it the anticipation of a future that included unambiguous acceptance of African Americans as equal partners in citizenship.

In *Federalist* 2, John Jay, seeking to portray the advantages of federal union, evoked "one connected, fertile, widespreading country," blessed with fertile soil, watered with innumerable streams and noble rivers. And this Edenic territory was, in his mind, populated by a united people, "descended from the same ancestors, speaking the same language, professing the same religion, attached to the same principles of government." The America Jay imagined may or may not have ever existed; what is less doubtful is its irrelevance to our contemporary predicament.

Political unity, not cultural unity, has always been the principal aspiration of the American polity. When wave after wave of immigrants reached the American shore, the new arrivals were anxious to become American citizens, not to abandon their cultural, religious, and ethnic backgrounds. And yet, as the essays in this volume illustrate in different ways, our understanding today of the meaning of our "unum" is evolving. The political union that we constitute may be becoming less separate from the pluralist cultural fabric of the nation than it once was. As Michael Walzer proposed a dozen years ago, the American government may find itself adapting to new notions of pluralism and to new expectations of cultural groups. Indeed, it may find itself using state power on behalf of those groups.

Some observers, like Robert Dahl, diagnose a weakened commitment to the common good—the result of rampant egotism and materialism, a decline in civic virtue, and a flight from citizenship to selfishness. Others, like Nathan Glazer, see the notion of a common good changing to recognize and even celebrate different groups. While pluralism and an ideal of tolerance of diversity stand in opposition to John Jay's image of a homogeneous America, Jay's loving image of America—at least in its depiction of a principled source of nationhood—is not shattered by the realities of American pluralism; rather it has been enriched by them. The heritage of the Enlightenment—its simultaneous valorization of universalist principles and of homogeneous nation-states—is being reinterpreted in American society at the end of the twentieth century. Whether this reinterpretation will lead to a deeper universalism, more subtle notions of freedom and equality, more probing conceptualizations of the pursuit of happiness, and broader notions of citizen and nation, remains to be seen.

1

Is Civic Virtue a Relevant Ideal in a Pluralist Democracy?

by Robert A. Dahl

In reflecting on the problem of the public good in a pluralist democracy it may be helpful to imagine three different possibilities for political life in a democratic country. Before describing them, however, let me offer several cautions. For one, the possibilities I am going to describe are highly schematic—too schematic, certainly, to capture the complexities of any specific political system, past, present, or, in all probability, future. For another, although my threefold typology might be applied to nondemocratic regimes, here I intend only to describe possibilities in countries with democratic political systems—or, perhaps I should say, with more or less democratic systems.

I

The first possibility might be called the politics of civic virtue. Here political life is truly extraordinary, even heroic. Here citizens engage in political life with the primary goal of achieving the public good, or the general welfare, or the good of all, or the public interest. Using an older form of political discourse we could say, then, that citizens are animated by the quality of civic virtue. Whatever qualities they may exhibit in their private and personal lives, in public life citizens are highly dedicated and willing, if need be, to undertake sacrifices in behalf of the public good.

This conception of a political order in which the political conduct of citizens, and certainly their leaders, is guided by a powerful and deeply

1

instilled sense of civic virtue has a long and impressive intellectual history originating with the political philosophers of classical Greece, notably Aristotle, and continuing in the active discourse of political thinkers through the American Revolution and beyond. In the last several decades, the ancient notion of a republic governed by the spirit and practice of civic virtue has been revived among historians and political theorists, who locate it not only in Aristotelian thought but also in the idea of civic humanism that was one element in the revival of classical ideals in Italy during the Renaissance. Because of its historical association with the idea of republican government, the centrality of civic virtue is also attributed to what is sometimes referred to as classical republicanism—spelled, I hasten to add, with a small *r* and bearing no perceptible relation, historical or otherwise, to the American political party bearing that name.

To achieve this extraordinary form of political life requires extraordinary conditions. For one thing, citizens and leaders must not be sharply divided into groups with conflicting goals—into associations competing with one another for the support and loyalties of citizens and making partial (one might say, partisan) demands on the state. Thus to many classical republicans—Rousseau, for example—the very existence of political associations was such an anathema that they would be forbidden in a well-ordered republic. Rousseau's ideal republic, we might say, was monistic, not pluralistic.

In more schematic a fashion than classical republicans would have put it, for an ideal republic to exist, either no political associations must exist—Rousseau's view in the *Social Contract*—or, if they do exist, then they must all be devoted to the general good and not to particularistic interests. And, of course, political parties would be an unmitigated evil with no place in a proper republic. In the Venetian republic, which was much admired in the seventeenth and eighteenth centuries by writers sympathetic with classical republican ideas, the laws and constitution actually made it illegal for citizens to form political associations.

This view of political associations and corresponding respect for the aristocratic Venetian republic was, incidentally, initially shared by many of the Framers of the American Constitution—until they learned from hard experience that political parties, legislative caucuses, and party organizations on the local, town, ward, city, state, and national levels were not only inescapable in the large democratic republic they had helped to establish, but even desirable.

Now if divisive political associations are to be avoided, citizens must be animated by more than a desire for the public good. They must also substantially agree on what *constitutes* the public good: what it is, its actual content, the substantive policies needed to achieve it. Too often, now as well as in earlier times, the public good is described in such general terms as to be empty of concrete meaning. After all, every citizen could claim—and in practice a great many do—that what he or she wants would truly be for the good of all. But if the public good is to have any relevance for political life, its content must be clearly specifiable. Consequently, although the implication is not often made explicit, the public good must be objective and knowable, or at any rate it must be so clear and self-evident that reasonable people are pretty certain to agree on it.

Let me remark in passing that I have run into more than a few persons who appear to believe this to be the case. They evidently believe that the public good *is* clear and self-evident, that *they* know what it is, and that it is exactly what *they* urge upon the government and their fellow citizens. Often, I find, people with this view also conclude that those who disagree with them must be either fools or knaves—blockheads who just can't understand what is perfectly obvious to any thinking person or selfish louts who simply do not care a whit about the public good. Theirs is not exactly the spirit of civility.

A democratic republic of dedicated virtuous citizens would also require a strong and focused political culture (to use our modern jargon) that not only inculcates citizens with a deep and informed loyalty to democratic ideals, values, practices, and institutions, but also instills them with the habits and outlooks necessary to civic virtue. But a political culture can hardly stand alone, independent of the broader culture in which it is embedded. So the general culture of our republic would need to instill in citizens a strong attachment to their community and the values of a shared, cooperative, and nonadversarial community life.

These considerations suggest further that the ideal republic might require an economic order and property arrangements that would support, or at least not impede, the development of a political and general culture supportive of civic virtue along the lines I have just described. Exactly what these arrangements would be is not clear to me, but I am inclined to think that our republic of civic virtue would find it difficult to exist with an economic and social order that generated highly individualistic, strongly materialist, competitive, and consumerist orientations and strivings. The classical advocates of republican government may have been on to something when, like Montesquieu, they assumed that a distinctive and necessary quality of citizens in a republic would

be their frugality. Opulence, they believed, was better suited to aristoc-
racies.

One more requirement seems evident, and it is exceptionally severe.
A democratic republic of virtuous citizens could hardly exist except
among a body of people so homogeneous in their conceptions of their
interests that sharply conflicting and partial views of the public good
would not arise, or if they did would be quickly and overwhelmingly
dismissed by a preponderant majority of citizens. It pretty much follows, therefore, that our ideal republic would have to be very small. For
an empirical matter, an increase in the number of persons or the amount
of territory included in a state—often, of course, both occur together—
almost invariably is accompanied by an increase in diversity. To say
essentially the same thing in another way, an increase in the scale of a
political system is likely to be accompanied by a decline in homogeneity, an increase in the number and variety of groups and subcultures,
and an increase in the likelihood of conflicts. If the politics of civic
virtue could exist anywhere, it seems, it could only be in a very small
republic.

Surprising as it may seem, whether a republic could exist at all except
on a very small scale was still highly debatable, and much debated, as
late as the American Revolution and the Constitutional Convention. The
entirely new kind of republican government and politics that resulted
from the Revolution and the Convention was not clearly foreseen, even
by the ablest minds of the time. As it turned out, that new kind of
republic made the ideal of civic virtue espoused by the classical republicans and the civic humanists impossible to achieve.

II

Lest you think my judgment too harsh, let me suggest some reasons
why I think the idealized portrait of political possibilities I have just
sketched out is impossible to attain in a large, modern, pluralistic, democratic country.

I have already introduced a problem that I have long thought to be
both fascinating and surprisingly neglected, namely, the problem of size
or scale. The ideals of civic virtue, civic humanism, and classical republicanism were all formulated by persons who had in mind the idealized
experience of very small states except for Rome. The city-states of classical Greece and medieval and Renaissance Italy were by today's standards tiny city-states—with few exceptions no larger than the modern

microstates of the Caribbean and Pacific islands. By classical standards, the citizen body of even a small country like Denmark would be considered gigantic.

Yet even though the older democracies and republics were predominantly microstates with comparatively small populations to begin with, they reduced the size of their citizen bodies still further by limiting citizenship to only a part, often a very small part, of all adults. In practice and in ideal, republics were small cities with tiny citizen bodies.

The main exceptions reveal how the attempt to adapt the classical ideals to states constructed on a more grandiose scale failed to confront the inherent difficulties. As Rome expanded from city-state to empire, it still maintained the political and constitutional forms of the city-state, thus effectively depriving an ever-increasing share of its citizens and subjects of genuine opportunities to participate in public life. Like the Greeks whom they ultimately subjected to their rule, the Romans failed to accept, and found it hard to conceive, that if the ideals of republican government were to survive on the colossal scale of expanding Rome, the citizen assemblies of the city-state would have to be displaced by bodies of elected representatives. As for the Venetian republic, although in both area and population it was large in comparison with other Italian republics, its citizen body was severely restricted to the male members of a hereditary aristocracy who always numbered less than two thousand.

It is worth remembering that small as they were, the citizen bodies in the older democracies and republics were hardly so homogeneous as to be free of severe political conflicts. Indeed, actual politics was pretty far removed from the ideal. On such evidence as is available to me, I seriously doubt that political life in the city-states, including Athens, was on the whole notably superior to our own. Not infrequently politics was harsh, brutal, factional, and quite literally lethal. Reflecting on his reading of the histories of small states, James Madison concluded that factionalism had been the very bane of republics. In a speech at the Constitutional Convention and later in the now famous Number 10 of *The Federalist*, Madison boldly turned the ancient argument upside down by contending that the cure for factions was to *increase* the size of republics, thereby increasing the number and diversity of factions and by so doing insuring that no single faction would be likely to prevail. Though I have some doubts about his inference, his interpretation of historical experience and his pluralist vision of politics were, I believe, essentially sound.

To repeat, whatever we may conclude about the older city-state republics, democratic countries today contain too much diversity to make it possible for citizens to sustain the degree of agreement on the substance of the public good that the older ideal required.

The large scale of political society creates another closely related problem: the relative strength of egoism and altruism in human behavior. I want to propose a sort of law of diminishing returns to virtue from group size, a kind of reverse analogue to the economists' idea of increasing returns from scale. The law might be stated roughly as follows: The greater the number of persons in a group, the more that civic virtue requires altruism, and yet the weaker the force of altruism. Let me explain. If you are a member of a small group of people knitted together by strong bonds formed from family ties, friendship, history, and shared experiences, you may feel that the best interests of the group are your own as well. Egoism merges indistinguishably with altruism. And even on occasions when some of your interests diverge from those of others, you may readily sacrifice your interests for the good of all: in short, you behave altruistically. Altruistic behavior among human beings is far more common in the world, I believe, than cynics assume. But almost all altruism occurs in small, usually very small, groups. The prototypical example is, of course, the family. As the group expands in numbers, as homogeneity declines, and as conflicting interests increase, for you to sacrifice your own interests to the general good requires an ever-increasing scope for your altruism. Yet as your group grows in numbers, the bonds of love, affection, and solidarity among you weaken: more and more of the others are strangers, unknown to you, distant from you physically, psychologically, socially. Our grief over the death of one person we deeply love is immeasurable. Yet the emotion created by a three-inch news item reporting the death of thousands in a flood in Bangladesh will be all but undetectable among those of us whose close ties embrace not a single victim. If the very nature of human emotions impedes altruism, so does the very nature of our cognitive capacities: our brains, our central nervous systems, our minds, our awareness. For so little do we know about the uncountable distant others that we often find it impossible even to know what is in their best interests. The obstacles to altruism, we might say, are not only affective but cognitive as well. For we are not ants or bees, bound together by instinct and learning in a vast cooperative super-organism that evolution has beautifully designed for species survival.

Must we conclude, then, that the heroic altruism required for a politics of civic virtue is never possible in a large political society? Not quite. Yet I think it may be possible only during profound emergencies that threaten survival—in the past, mainly war and acute economic crisis. Thus it is not surprising, though perhaps slightly ironic, that the most recent examples of a willingness to sacrifice and a selfless dedication to the public good have appeared during transitions from dictatorships toward the inauguration or restoration of democracy, when a new and beautiful world is just over the horizon and nobility in rhetoric is sometimes matched by a nobility in action. Alas, the public soon wearies of its own nobility; it wants order, stability, food, jobs, family life, and a future. Leaders who had selflessly devoted themselves to achieving the democratic institutions they so much admired now confront the prosaic and sometimes bitter politics of everyday life, and realize that they must either acquire the skills such politics need or step aside for those who have them.

In his Categorical Imperative, Kant, like Jesus in his Sermon on the Mount, formulated a lofty, demanding, and noble standard for how we ought to act. But human experience tells us that we generally do not obey that Imperative, and the more persons we include in the scope of the Imperative, the less likely we are to obey it. We may wish that human beings were highly altruistic in their conduct toward distant and unknown others. Yet as the Framers of the American Constitution well knew, it would be folly to design a political society on the assumption that they will be. Here is what the greatest American political scientist wrote in a letter to a lifelong friend:

> Those who contend for a simple Democracy, or a pure Republic, actuated by the sense of the majority, and operating within narrow limits, assume or suppose a case which is altogether fictitious. They found their reasoning on the idea, that the people composing the Society, enjoy not only an equality of political rights; but that they have all precisely the same interests, and the same feelings in every respect. Were this in reality the case, their reasoning would be conclusive. The interest of the majority would be that of the minority also; the decisions could only turn on mere opinion concerning the good of the whole, of which the major voice would be the safest criterion; and within a small sphere, the voice could be most easily collected, and the public affairs most accurately managed.

Then our political scientist concludes with this devastating judgment:

> We know however that no Society ever did or can consist of so homogeneous a mass of citizens.[1]

These wise words were written by James Madison in October 1787 to Thomas Jefferson in Paris.

III

Let me mention briefly two other problems, which can be boiled down to saying that both terms in the expression *public good*—and in related expressions—are highly ambiguous to say the least. We tend to speak of the *public* good as if we had a definite, well-circumscribed, and relevant public in view. So it might be in a small city-state, though in practice the well-being of many of the residents of the city-state was excluded from serious consideration simply because, like women, slaves, and foreigners in Athens, they had no political voice. In a pluralist society and a pluralist world, we may have concerns for the good of innumerable publics that are not all well bounded, are sometimes overlapping, and quite likely have conflicting needs, wants, goals, interests. So in thinking about the public good, we need to ask: the public good of which public?

Finally, philosophical inquiry in the past century has pretty well knocked the props out from under the assumption that rational people must necessarily arrive at an agreed understanding of an objective, knowable good, whether for all times and places or just here and now. An assertion that such and such is in the public good runs smack into the question: how can you demonstrate rationally that such and such is good? Any attempt to answer the question will be, as some philosophers put it, fundamentally contestable. You and I might agree that such and such is good, either generally or in a specific situation. But unless one of us turns out to be more creative than any philosopher in this century, neither of us would be capable of demonstrating that our agreement is rationally justified. This suggests the possibility that we should be less concerned about proving decisively what is good and more concerned about how we might reach agreement on what is good, or, if we cannot, how we may live together with civility and mutual understanding.

IV

You might well wonder, however, whether a political life of decency and civility is possible. One answer, which is as ancient and persistent as the idea of civic virtue, is a flat-out no. Versions of this answer are expressed by Thrasymachus in Plato's *Republic*,[2] by Machiavelli in *The Prince*, by Hobbes in *The Leviathan*, and by your average American citizen in discussing Congress. In this view, politics is inescapably a contest among egoists who selfishly pursue their own interests, whether power, prestige, wealth, security, all of these, or something else. Over against the ideal of civic virtue is the empirical inevitability, so it is said, of a politics of hyper-egoism.

I find it interesting that during essentially the same period when some scholars have held up the politics of civic virtue as a model, others have held up the politics of hyper-egoism as a model. I have in mind recent theories of rational choice that purport to describe and explain politics as rational choices by actors pursuing their own interests. The first is a model in the more conventional sense: it is meant only partly to be descriptive of certain previous political systems and even more to be a relevant ideal. Rational choice models, however, are portrayed—in the spirit of Thrasymachus, Machiavelli, and Hobbes—as strictly empirical: not descriptions of what ought to be but of what is and must be. If Thrasymachus and company are right, then for you to contend that politics ought to meet higher moral standards is simply irrelevant moralizing, rather like making moral judgments about a volcanic explosion. For to Thrasymachus and company, the world is what it is and will be, not what you wish it were, or might be, or ought to be.

To the politics of hyper-egoism described in nonmathematical form by Thrasymachus and company, recent rational choice theories appear to provide a modern, empirical, hard-nosed, incontestably scientific foundation. On inspection, however, these seemingly rigorously scientific theories prove to be deeply, even fatally, flawed. As Robert Lane has shown, empirical evidence demonstrates that rational choice does not even satisfactorily explain behavior in the one area of human life for which it is surely most suitable—economic life.[3] What is more, as Ian Shapiro and Donald Green demonstrate, the scientific pretensions of rational choice models are vastly exaggerated. The models, they show, typically suffer from one of three defects: Either they are not rigorously tested against empirical evidence, which is to say they are mathematical exercises that take only a casual glance at the real world. Or, in the rare cases when they are actually tested, the findings are trivial. Or, the *coup de grace*, when they are tested and findings are nontrivial, they fail to confirm the model and may even falsify it.[4]

Nonetheless, although I am extremely doubtful about the validity of existing rational choice theory as a description of political life, the views of Thrasymachus and company cannot be dismissed. The politics of hyper-egoism does exist in the real world, and it is a standing danger to the potentiality for decent politics in a democratic system.

Let me portray the politics of hyper-egoism as a kind of polar antithesis to the politics of civic virtue. In the place of virtue, egoism; in the place of the public good, the citizen's own interests. Dedication and willingness to sacrifice? Yes, though not to the public good but to one's own interests. Political associations? Yes, but devoted exclusively to their own narrow goals. Political parties? Yes, but with hyper-egoism having rendered them incapable of reconciling the panoply of interests into mutually beneficial coalitions; instead of integrating, they fragment public life into conflicting segments. A supporting political culture? Yes, indeed, but a culture of political cynicism, of noncommitment, in which selfish striving is the accepted norm, and to appear to work for the public good is viewed as hypocrisy or stupidity. Nobility? No. Venality? Yes.

The broader culture of the society in turn strengthens individual and group identities and loyalties at the expense of identification with a loyalty to the nation or the country.

What conditions of economic life would help to support the politics of hyper-egoism? The answer presents a paradox that I do not have time to explore here. The only countries in which democratic institutions have developed into stable systems are countries with capitalist economies and largely competitive markets; yet the culture and practices of capitalism favor egoism over altruism and the pursuit of private good over public good. However, despite the claims of that rapidly vanishing though not yet extinct species, orthodox Marxists, capitalist economies are not all the same and relations between politics and the economy are not the same in all capitalist countries. Political life in Norway and Sweden, for example, is not political life in Japan and Italy.

The politics of hyper-egoism is favored, I would think, by two very different kinds of economic conditions. One is persistent lack of economic growth, or even decline: for without a surplus to share, politics is zero sum: I gain, you lose, you lose, I gain. Some observers have so described Argentine political life during its earlier democratic interludes between Peronism and military dictatorship. (Fortunately, a growing economy may be changing the political culture of that now democratic country.) The other and very different pattern, illustrated by Italy and Japan, actually combines a high rate of economic growth with hyper-egoism in political life. This combination is achieved by turning elections and parliamentary politics into a side show financially subsidized by business. In Japan, government economic policies and programs have been formulated and carried out by what amounted to an autonomous and highly meritocratic bureaucracy pretty much independent of elections, party maneuvers, and parliament. Until the decimation of the Italian political class by scandal and judicial process, Italy was governed by a kleptocracy drawn from the leading members of the governing parties. In both countries—more extensively in Italy, it seems, than in Japan—the political class used and was used by major criminal organizations.[5] In fact, in Sicily and parts of Southern Italy, criminal societies have effectively acquired considerable control over the state itself. In both countries, particularly in Italy, a wave of popular revulsion with the indecent, degraded, politics of hyper-egoism may help to bring changes about. Time will tell.

V

The politics of civic virtue is impossible; the politics of hyper-egoism is morally repulsive and sometimes self-destructive. If we cannot achieve the first, must we inevitably succumb to the second? I do not think so, even though we may not always escape some aspects of it. What I am going to call the politics of robust civility is an alternative to both. Although it needs less nobility than civic virtue requires, it provides more civility, decency, sympathy, and generosity of spirit than can be found in the politics of hyper-egoism. But by saying that civility is robust, I mean to emphasize that we ought not to expect, or even to desire, that politics be modeled on the decorum of the Pickwick Club. Strong dissent and disagreement are not just likely; they are often desirable. It is sometimes true, alas, that you cannot be heard unless you shout.

   Like its alternatives, the politics of robust civility also has distinguished intellectual forebears. Some of them may surprise you: they include Machiavelli—the Machiavelli of the *Discourses*—and Adam Smith—the Smith of *The Theory of Moral Sentiments*. We may also count Montesquieu in *The Spirit of the Laws* and, like Smith, other philosophers of the Scottish Enlightenment, notably David Hume and Adam Ferguson, both of whom greatly influenced James Madison. To this impressive list I would add Madison himself.

   Although I would not contend that this diverse group presented a common theory, I think they all might agree on the following propositions:

1. Human beings possess inborn capacities for acting not only from narrow self-interest but also from a concern for others. The most fundamental and universal human feelings include not only

selfishness but also sympathy. Egoists we often may be, but we are also capable of benevolence and sometimes even altruism.

2. How these human capacities are developed and expressed depends on individual character, on opportunities, on the way choices are structured, and on circumstances, accident, chance— Machiavelli's *Fortuna*.

3. Among the important influences on character, opportunities, and the structure of choices are human institutions, including political institutions. In shaping human character and action, institutions do matter. In fact they greatly matter.

4. Like other human institutions, political institutions are not always everywhere the same.

5. Given the appropriate institutions, it is possible to find citizens and leaders who are capable of creating and maintaining a politics of robust civility.

6. Although political institutions are not like clay that can be shaped and molded by the intentions of the sculptor, their shape and form are not wholly independent of human will and knowledge. If institutions shape human beings, human beings can also shape institutions.

Let me call these half dozen propositions the axiomatics of a politics of robust civility. These axiomatics, it is obvious, assume that human beings possess both limits and potentialities that are different from those assumed in the politics of civic virtue and the politics of hyperegoism. What is true of individuals is also true of groups and associations. Rousseau feared political associations and would have them prohibited. Like Rousseau, Madison, who was instrumental in replacing the old theory and practice of republican government with the new, feared what factional associations might do but thought them inevitable in a republic, and proposed to limit their potential for harming the general good by enlarging the size of the polity. When, however, Tocqueville visited the United States in 1832 he was astonished at the plethora of associations, political, educational, economic, and other, to which Americans belonged. Contradicting Rousseau and qualifying Madison, he saw that a rich associational life within the larger republic could be a definite virtue, not a vice.

Central to the politics of robust civility is a special kind of political association that to Rousseau and his predecessors had no proper place in a republic—and of which, in fact, they had no clear conception. This is the much maligned political party. At their best, and obviously they are not often at their best, political parties can help to negotiate among the enormous variety of concerns, interests, goals, and demands of citizens, groups, associations, even subcultures to bring about compromises that achieve some part of what each seeks, at the least expense to the rest. At their best, then, they function to *integrate* conflicting demands into mutually beneficial compromises.

Does the politics of robust civility mean no more, then, than abandoning political ideals and accommodating ourselves to existing political life? Not at all. The politics of robust civility expresses values that may be less demanding than the politics of civic virtue but are far more demanding than the politics of hyper-egoism. To insist on the possibilities of attaining a politics of robust civility requires us to think of the public good less as substance and more as process.[6] Reinterpreted in this way, to exercise civic virtue is to do what we must to create and maintain the processes by which we as citizens can engage in a joint search for what is best. In a large pluralistic republic a virtuous citizen would, I believe, add more propositions to the axioms I described earlier:

- To disagree is human. Every human being experiences and interprets the world, in part at least, in a unique way. This uniqueness is an essential and inescapable element of what it means to be human. Yet because resources and opportunities are finite and limited, one person's choices and ends often conflict with those of another. Thus the uniqueness of human beings is both a fundamental value and a fundamental problem.
- Although we cannot rationally demonstrate that one end or set of ends is always or even generally good or best, it does not follow that all choices are equally good or desirable. People can be mistaken in their choices. Each of us sometimes makes and acts upon choices that, after experiencing and reflecting upon the consequences, we regret having made and, were it possible, we would undo. But we cannot undo choices we have made and acted upon. We can only try to undo some of the consequences and to avoid or at least minimize our mistaken choices in the future.
- Moreover, before we make and act upon choices we can sometimes reflect on the likelihood and consequences of different outcomes. Given optimal conditions, we can enrich these reflections with the best information available. We can act upon an enlightened understanding of our situation and the choices it allows. From this perspective, we might say that a person's good or interest is whatever

that person would choose, given the fullest attainable understanding of the experience resulting from that choice and its most relevant alternatives.[7]

- Frequently, however, we cannot make our choices effective except by acting in concert with others, with the implicit or explicit understanding that we will abide by the decision we make collectively.

- Although frequently we cannot agree on what is best and our preferred choice is in conflict with that of others, sometimes we can agree with others on what constitutes the best *process* for arriving at collective decisions. We may sometimes agree that the best process should both satisfy tests of fairness and encourage enlightened understanding. A fair process, we might further agree, would require that we treat one another as political equals. But if we are to treat one another as political equals, then enlightened understanding requires that each of us also engages in an effort to understand the choices and ends of the others. Robust civility requires more than speaking out, no matter how loudly; it also requires listening—and not merely listening but hearing.

- A process that leads to collective decisions based simply on *will* or raw uninformed *preference* is, then, neither fair to its participants nor enlightened. And, I would argue, such a process violates the very assumptions that justify democracy. A fair, enlightening, and democratic process would provide time and opportunity for learning, including learning from one another.

- Finally, a fair and enlightening process would exclude coercion, domination, manipulation, and influence resulting from superior access to such resources as money, control of information, and others. The consequences of this last requirement are far-reaching and might even be regarded by some as Utopian. Yet I do not see how we can treat one another as political equals if we permit our collective decisions to be determined by capacities extraneous to our qualities as citizens and human beings.

Admittedly what I have just described as the politics of robust civility is an ideal to which, so far as I am aware, no political system has ever fully measured up. However, I do think that some countries come closer to it than others. For whatever my judgment may be worth, if I were to locate democratic countries along a continuum extending from that ideal to the naked politics of hyper-egoism, I would be inclined to put the Scandinavian countries and Switzerland toward the one end, though certainly some distance from it, and Italy and Japan toward the other extreme, with the United States somewhere in between.

In providing us with an unattainable ideal the politics of robust civility is similar to the politics of civic virtue. But unlike the politics of civic virtue, robust civility is an appropriate aspiration for the time and circumstances in which we live. To citizens of a large pluralist democratic republic, it offers some relevant standards against which to appraise their failures, their achievements, and their yet unfulfilled possibilities.

Notes

1. Quoted in William Lee Miller, *The Business of May Next: James Madison and the Founding* (Charlottesville, Va.: University Press of Virginia, 1992), 148.

2. Callicles in the dialogue *Gorgias* could also be included in this distinguished company.

3. Robert E. Lane, *The Market Experience* (New York: Cambridge University Press, 1991).

4. Donald Green and Ian Shapiro, *Pathologies of Rational Choice Theory: A Critique of Applications in Political Science* (New Haven: Yale University Press, 1994).

5. I should point out that at the time of writing, in both countries public information about political corruption and criminality is drawn mostly from charges by prosecutors and magistrates. Whether all those charged will be found guilty in a court of law, or by judicious observers, remains to be seen.

6. I have dealt with this question at greater length in *Democracy and Its Critics* (New Haven: Yale University Press, 1989), in chapters 12, 13, and 20, "Process and Substance," "Process versus Process," and "Pluralism, Polyarchy, and the Common Good." Although they might not agree with all I say here, many other writers have advanced somewhat similar conceptions of what I call here the politics of robust civility. These include Bruce A. Ackerman, *Social Justice in the Liberal State* (New Haven: Yale University Press, 1980); Stuart Hampshire, "Liberalism: The New Twist," *The New York Review*, August 12, 1993, 43–44; J. Donald Moon, "Theory, Citizenship, and Democracy," in George E. Marcus and Russell L. Hanson, *Reconsidering the Democratic Public* (University Park, Pennsylvania: Pennsylvania State University Press, 1993), 211–22; and Donald R. Kinder and Don Herzog, "Democratic Discussion," in Marcus, *Reconsidering the Democratic Public*, 347–78. Although these writers are in the Anglo-American political tradition, the view set out here has been shared, at least in part, by advocates of democracy in other countries as well. In 1956 the Norwegian philosopher Arne Naess defined a

democratic system according to "the *quality of its public debate*." A decade earlier in 1945, in a pamphlet issued by the Danish resistance, a Danish theologian wrote that democracy "is not determined by taking a vote. Rather its essence can be seen more properly in deliberations, negotiations, in mutual respect and understanding and in the growing regard for the interests of the whole." (I am indebted to Bernt Hagtvet for these quotations.)

  7. For further discussion, see my *Democracy and Its Critics*, 306ff.

2

Lawyers as Citizens: An Inquiry into National Loyalty and the Professional Identity of Lawyers[1]

by Sanford Levinson[2]

An Encounter in Hungary

I begin with a June 1992 encounter in Hungary, during my participation in a seminar for Eastern European lawyers. I was teaching a sequence of classes on the American view of the legal profession. Eastern European lawyers, who were themselves participating in the design of institutional structures—including an organized bar—appropriate to the new political orders emerging in those countries, presumably might learn something from the American experience. Perhaps the most basic lesson of teaching, though, is that the learning process can work two ways, and it is not always easy to distinguish the teachers from the taught.

One of my central interests concerned the conditions that could be legitimately placed by the state on entry to the practice of law. Thus I presented several cases of the United States Supreme Court dealing with constitutional limitations to state regulation of the bar. For example, could a state limit membership in the bar to ''loyal Americans,'' defined as those untainted by contact with ''subversive'' ideas or by membership in organizations like the Communist Party? Several states had attempted just such limitations, and the Supreme Court delivered mixed responses when these limitations were challenged. However, the final outcome of these several cases was that states could not constitutionally use membership in the Communist Party per se as a bar to entry to the legal profession.[3] The state could *ask* about membership, and it could use answers as the basis for further conversation about the commitment to illegal goals of the party, such as working toward the violent overthrow of the American government. Anyone expressing such commitment *could* be kept out of the bar. However, simple party membership—and even support of the desirability of radical transformation of the polity into a proletarian dictatorship—would not be disqualifying.

The Hungarian, Ukranian, Georgian, Bulgarian, and other East European lawyers gathered together in a small town outside of Budapest expressed strong views regarding the state's duty to welcome professing Communists into the practicing bar. Most of them were were critical of current American constitutional doctrine regarding the rights of Communist lawyers. They tended to view American liberals like myself as almost laughably (or tragically) naive in our formal indifference to the political beliefs, including hostility to some basic norms of liberal democracy, of those who would enter the legal profession. They would scarcely entrust the bar to those whose ideological loyalties were suspect.

But, of course, overt ideology is only one example of the barriers to entry placed by the state on membership in the legal profession. I was also especially interested in another one, involving one's formal status as a member of the state. This, too, provoked considerable discussion, the most vigorous discussant being a Latvian, Imma Jansone, who was employed by the equivalent of the Latvian Bar Association. Although she had expressed her share of skepticism about welcoming Communists into the bar, the principal conflict between Ms. Jansone and me took place over a quite different case, *In re* Griffiths,[4] a 1973 decision of the Supreme Court striking down a Connecticut law limiting membership in the state bar to citizens of the United States.

Ms. Jansone vigorously disagreed with my support for the Court's decision, especially when I used it as the basis for suggesting that the Latvian and other East European bars should not restrict their membership to political nationals. Instead she defended the desire of the local bar to restrict legal practice in Latvia not only to those who could pass an examination demonstrating sufficient knowledge of Latvian law, an altogether reasonable limitation, but also to *citizens* of the newly revived country and speakers of its language. As we began our discussion, I assumed that we simply represented the conflict between my own (highly desirable) liberal universalism and her (quite dubious) tribal parochialism, especially if one assumes that emphasis on Latvian citizenship and linguistic abilities is a coded way of denying full rights to long-time (and, in many cases, life-time) Russian residents of Latvia who would be denied such citizenship.[5] As the discussion progressed, however, I realized that the situation may be more complex than I had first thought and that her position might be more defensible than I first thought. I then wondered whether the rationale for her position was substantially dependent on the specific circumstances of Latvia or, indeed, if it might have implications even for our own, very different, political and cultural situation here in the United States. What follows is an attempt to address these questions, which involves in turn nothing less than reflecting on the intersections, if any, of the duties of citizenship and the role played by the modern lawyers.

The Lawyer as Citizen and as Friend

Harvard Professor of Law Charles Fried began a famous article on "the moral foundations of the lawyer-client relationship" by asking, "Can a good lawyer be a good person?"[6] What if, for example, a lawyer worked to vindicate the legal rights of pornographers or of a landlord seeking eviction of a poor family for failure to pay the rent or, as I have done, of the Klu Klux Klan to march down the main street of the capital of Texas? Fried answered his question (and countered any such examples) with a resounding affirmation of the lawyer's role; in a reasonably just society, he argued, it is *always* morally admirable to help persons achieve *whatever* the law entitles them to do, even if the lawyers in question would choose to lead their own lives in considerably different ways from those of their clients.

Many critics have properly argued that Fried's question is surely too broad. Only the most rabid antilawyers have argued that the lawyer *cannot* be a good person, that it is enough to know that persons are lawyers in order to identify them as bad.[7] It is far more sensible to ask (something like), "To what extent, and under what circumstances, might the attributes of being a good lawyer and being a good person conflict?"

I thus adapt Fried's question as follows: Will a good lawyer, as defined by fidelity to the norms of professional conduct, necessarily be a good *citizen* as well? A negative answer means that one must then recognize potential distinctions between the attributes of (professionally honorable) lawyering and of citizenship. Someone identified by standard American professional norms as a first-rate lawyer would at the same time be potentially describable as a questionable, even bad, citizen.

A full exploration of this question would require nothing less than elaboration of the notions both of good lawyering and of good citizenship. The latter, in particular, would have to be distinguished from what might be termed mere citizenship, i.e., the possession of an external legal status as a citizen of a given polity that, however, is not significantly intertwined with some internal, phenomenological sense of strong political identity and commitment to shared political purposes. Mere citizens may be similar to what Michael Walzer once described as "alienated residents," who may live within a formal political space, but for whom that status has almost no affective meaning.[8]

I turn once more to Fried's article, which turned substantially on a metaphor of the lawyer as the client's "friend." According to Fried, "like a friend [your lawyer] acts in your interests, not his own; or rather he adopts your interests as his own. I would call that the classic definition of friendship."[9] Whatever the problems with Fried's metaphor of the lawyer as the client's friend—one does not, for example, often hire one's friends—they do not preclude us from adopting it in regard to the role of the citizen, where it may prove considerably more illuminating.

What do we mean when we describe someone as a *good* citizen, as distinguished, presumably, not only from a *bad* citizen, but even from a Walzerian *mere* citizen, who may live within a polity but for whom that status has no affective meaning? I suggest that we are evoking someone who is, in some sense, a genuine friend of the polity, devoted to its interests and willing, if necessary, to subordinate more selfish individual interests to those of the polity. A traditional name for this kind of citizenship is, of course, patriotism. As Francis Lieber, an important 19th century writer, wrote, "Without patriotism . . . all must dissolve into dreary, heartless egoism. But even to regret such an occurrence and strive to prevent it requires patriotism."[10]

Some versions of such civil friendship are almost frightening in their monomania, such as Rousseau's stunning invocation in *Emile* of the Spartan mother who, upon being told by a messenger that her five sons had just died in a battle, responded, "You fool. Did we win the battle or not?" Most of us probably find this exemplary not of friendship but of totalitarianism inasmuch as it seems to diminish any loyalties and attachments other than civic ones. But are we really forced to choose either Spartan totalitarianism or celebration of a desiccated notion of citizenship whose sole meaning in effect becomes the possession of rights *against* the state without any concern for *duties* owed it as well? I think not. And, of course, I am not alone. Much contemporary thought, whether high academic political theory or books written for more general audiences, criticizes an unalloyed rights-centeredness and proclaims the importance of communal interests as well, even as one of these interests is the preservation of a respect for pluralism and traditional civil liberties.[11]

In this context I am reminded of the Connecticut oath, now going back over 350 years, that is taken by new voters. They must "solemnly swear" to "be true and faithful to the state of Connecticut, and to the constitution and the government, thereof . . . and to the constitution of the United States." More to the point, "whenever you are called upon to give your vote or choice touching any matter which concerns this state or the United States, you will do this in a manner which you shall judge contributes to the best interests of Connecticut and the nation, without respect or favor of any person," including the person of oneself.[12] At least some of the older readers of this essay might also remember President Kennedy's famous plea to the citizenry to "ask not what your country can do for you; ask what you can do for your country."

More is involved in good citizenship than merely obeying the laws, just as, presumably, more is required to be a good parent than simply refraining from child abuse. Both practices, to earn commendation, require a disposition of concern and care for others, including a willingness, when necessary, to subordinate one's own desires or interests to others (even as children must learn in turn that parents have their own legitimate desires and interests that must be recognized). Of course, the purpose is to create a community, whether we call it the polity or the family, that enjoys a status quite different from simply a collection of the discrete individuals counted as its members. One of the things that characterizes such communities, presumably, is the existence of "bonds of sympathy" among its members "despite the differences of opinion that set them apart on questions concerning the ends, and hence the identity, of their community," a condition that Dean Anthony Kronman of the Yale Law School labels "political fraternity."[13]

I am, therefore, ultimately interested in the extent to which, in the words of the sociologist Stephen Cohen, "professions are potential communities; and, as such, they might serve as surrogates and replacements" for other, more typical, kinds of communities. Cohen even suggests that "some professions could conceivably rival ethnic and religious communities in many ways."[14] Interestingly enough, Cohen does not list "political communities" among the potential competitors for feelings of loyalty and commitment. Is it possible, though, that the professional community—and adherence to its norms—could even become a rival, in some significant sense, to the polity? Should that be the case, is it a cause for worry, or might we view such professional communities as just one more tile of a mosaic celebrating cultural pluralism and the presence of mediating institutions that can resist the imperial claims of the state, which is put in its place, so to speak, as only *one* among a number of equally legitimate contenders for a person's individual loyalties?[15]

No one familiar with contemporary American culture can avoid the issue of multiculturalism and the ostensible challenges posed by cultural fragmentation to standard notions of social and political unity. Multiculturalism comes in many different disguises, though. It may be that the potential conflicts generated by cultures of professionalism are as important as those caused by more typical racial, ethnic, or religious identities, even if, to be sure, it is these latter problems that are more likely to eventuate in bloodshed. Moreover, to focus on fragmentation may be misleading if it suggests that the only threat to national unity comes from *sub*-communities within the territorial polity. One might also note the possibility of *transnational* loyalties that go beyond the nation-state. The most obvious example is the Roman Catholic Church. One might wonder, then, if the ever-growing internationalization of the legal profession will also lead to a cross-national professional identity that is significantly independent of the national identity provided by the passport that a particular lawyer happens to carry. And, to the extent that that occurs, should it be something to applaud or to fear?

What Do Lawyers Do?

Answering any of these questions and determining the merits of the state's limiting membership in the profession to citizens require that one have an image of what it is that lawyers do (as well, as already suggested, as what it is that citizens do). A central task of my sojourn in Hungary, therefore, was elaborating to the Eastern Europeans a description of how American lawyers conceptualized their own role and described their own activities. To this end I assigned the seminal 1897 speech by Oliver Wendell Holmes, *The Path of the Law*.[16] Holmes's speech is, I believe, the most important discussion of the legal profession ever penned by an American, not least because of its decidedly unsentimental view of the lawyer's role.

Speaking to law students at Boston University about the vocation they had chosen, Holmes asks them to reflect on the central task of the ordinary lawyer. Is it, for example, the careful study of norms of justice or the social good and the conveying to clients the results of such study? Not really. Sweeping aside any traditional notion of the lawyer as a civic-republican patriot, Holmes replaces it with the image of a businessman selling a very specific commodity, which is knowledge about the actual behavior of public officials who possess the capacity to bring public force to bear on one's clients. The business of the lawyer is simply the prediction of the likely behavior of public officials, particularly judges, in response to the acts of citizens. Law is ascertained through acute observation of political behavior—experience—rather than produced by dazzling logical analyses that might be altogether irrelevant to the actual behavior found within the society under examination. This means, among other things, a strict analytical separation between description and assessment—that is, between law and morality. Holmes leaves no doubt that the role of the lawyer is to purvey accurate descriptive accounts to clients who will then base their behavior on the desire to avoid unfortunate encounters with, and the costs imposed by, public authority.

Holmes conveys a decidedly skeptical overtone about the moral status of public authority. Although he had suffered three separate wounds during the great struggle of 1861–65 that so tested the meaning of American citizenship in our own history, he viewed life by-and-large as a relentless struggle among brutally contending competitors, with survival being its own justification. Law itself was simply an assertion of power, and the lawyer's role was to be the detached purveyor of a certain kind of information about the likely use of public force.

The skilled lawyer knows that there exists the ''law in action'' that differs from the conceptual clarification of what Roscoe Pound, an important contemporary of Holmes, somewhat disdainfully dismissed as the mere ''law on the books.'' The law on the books may in fact be utterly ignored by most public officials and thus, as a practical matter, be without force. Holmes described, and some would even say he helped to create, a client who wants simply to know, concretely, what is likely to happen upon a certain course of conduct. An important analytical construct developed by Holmes is that of the bad man, who is motivated only to avoid unpleasant consequences but not concerned, for example, to do good, however defined, for its own sake.

Holmes by no means suggested that one should avoid representing such bad men. Indeed, bad men would comprise much of the market for the services that Holmesian lawyers had to sell, because their own behavior was the product not of an internal moral compass but, rather, of the simple desire to avoid actions whose costs would outweigh their benefits. The lawyer who serves such a client is basically indifferent to the use that will be made by the client of the information provided by the lawyer.

Not everyone accepts the Holmesian account. Dean Kronman has recently offered the important analysis—part jeremiad, part call to action—of the legal profession that is strikingly anti-Holmesian in its thrust. Far from the lawyer as detached predictor, Kronman's lawyer is an embedded member of a particular political community, sharing this identity with his or her clients and with the judges who will decide their cases.[17] This embeddedness, among other things, generates the attribute of statesmanship that for Kronman defines legal practice at its best. For Kronman, "the good lawyer does care about the soundness of the legal order. . . . He shares the judge's public-spirited devotion to it."[18] Similar argument can be found in Robert Gordon's classic neo-republican essay *The Independence of Lawyers*,[19] which, as the title suggests, calls on lawyers to maintain some independence from the client and to see themselves as potential moral teachers of those clients.

As Kronman himself admits (and bewails), the lawyer as statesman is perhaps under fatal assault for reasons ranging from internal developments within American legal education to the modern culture of the large law firm. Still, there may be at least some citizen-lawyers who practice in the United States and feel some identification with the polity and its interests. But what about those multinational lawyers who practice law outside their polities? What precisely would it mean for *them* to be statesmen or republicans, neo or otherwise? After all, what polity or social order would they identify with? Consider in this context U.S. Secretary of Labor Robert Reich's emphasis on the relationship between national attachments and the inculcation of a necessary spirit of self-sacrifice. "We learn to feel responsible for others," says Reich, "because we share with them a common history . . . a common culture . . . a common fate." He is therefore at least somewhat wary of the the "darker side of [the] cosmopolitanization" represented by multinational enterprise insofar as it generates persons who identify themselves as "world citizens, but without accepting . . . any of the obligations that citizenship in a [particular] polity normally implies."[20]

How might this tension between the Holmesian and Kronmanian visions of legal practice be relevant to Eastern Europeans concerned with constructing radically new political orders—or how even to us as Americans, the sons and daughters of Holmes but perhaps fearful, like Kronman (and many others), of many of the features we see when observing our contemporary society? One answer is as follows: To the extent that members of the general society, including lawyers, restrict their operative definition of law to the actual behavior of public officials in enforcing the law, then a state concerned with legal compliance must invest far more resources in enforcement procedures than might otherwise be the case.

Why is this so? The answer is that the state simply cannot rely on its Holmesian members to feel a sufficient sense of moral obligation to obey the abstract commands of the state even in the absence of the credible threat of public force. To be sure, some citizens, as was presumably the case in pre-1989 Eastern Europe, might be tempted to reject the commands of the state because of a belief that the state was itself significantly—and illegitimately—detached from the underlying community. Others, more atomistic, might be equally disdainful of community as well as state, viewing both as reifications threatening the playing out of individual desire.

Whatever the underlying social or theoretical basis, however, public officials looking at the members of a Holmesian society, including (presumably) its lawyers, will see not "citizens" asking questions about public interest (and obligations) as much as egoists trying simply to maximize their self-interest. The commands of the state are viewed simply as expressions of desired conduct; they are otherwise without any genuine obligatory force. Legal "duties" are transformed into simple "prices" extracted for the conduct in question. There is a striking similarity between Holmes's view and that of Georg Lukacs, a Hungarian who was one of the leading Communist social theorists of this century. While describing a "total, communist fearlessness with regard to the state and the law," Lukacs asserted that "the law and its calculable consequences are of no greater (if also of no smaller) importance than any other external fact of life with which it is necessary to reckon when deciding upon any definite course of action." He compares the legal commands of the state with a train schedule: "The risk of breaking the law should not be regarded any differently than the risk of missing a train connection when on an important journey."[21] Thus, presumably, a lawyer is like a travel agent, although instead of train schedules the lawyer offers the client accurate information about actual odds of various official responses to the client's activity. The client is no more interested in the lawyer's view as to the "best" interpretation of the law, independent of the likelihood of that view really being enforced by officials with power, than are most clients interested in having the travel agent insist that they really ought to travel to some place different from the destination chosen by the client.

I don't want to sound overly critical of the Holmesian (or Lukacsian) attitude. It surely describes the actual way almost all of us live our lives on many occasions, as can be easily demonstrated by observing the responses of most of us to posted speed limits. Almost no one behaves as if 55 means 55 (and that disbelief is not merely the result of adherence to some fancy theory of linguistic indeterminacy). For most of us, 55 means something like 63, and I suspect it would mean 75–80 if we were confident that the state police would not stop anyone short of such speeds. And, presumably, what would lead many of us to make 80 mph the limit would be a calculation about the risks of accident and injury to ourselves as much as a focus on the increased risks borne by those sharing the highways with us.

Many of us have engaged in similarly predictive analyses of the law in regard to such subjects as sex, alcohol, and drugs. A Holmesian analysis also explains why most "good Americans" feel no compunctions about participating in various World Series, Super Bowl, or Final Four office pools even though they almost undoubtedly violate the "letter" of many states' laws prohibiting public gambling.[22] (And phone calls to out-of-state friends to make friendly bets bring one into violation of federal criminal law.) The tension between "law on the books" and "law in action" was, I think, at the heart of the controversy generated by President Clinton's initial nomination of Zoë Baird to be attorney general. Many of her defenders plausibly viewed the laws on the books about private individuals hiring illegal aliens as honored more in the breach than the observance: why should a prospective attorney general, unlike the rest of us, be without blemish in regard to fidelity to legal formalities?[23] Some of the same tensions may be present in regard to the actual behavior we expect from those who administer toxic dumps or run savings and loan organizations; at this point, of course, we may start worrying and begin asking about the possibility of encouraging a sense of genuinely shared destiny and membership in a social order as a way of taming more egoistic, asocial impulses.

Let us now return, at least figuratively, to Latvia.[24] In particular, I ask you to imagine a foreign investor in Latvia motivated simply by a desire to maximize profits. I am assuming, that is, that the investor has no particular commitment to the welfare of Latvia; any contribution to general Latvian welfare will, as suggested by classical economics, be only a happy byproduct of the quest for private gains, and not the motivation for the investor's behavior. So long as these gains are sufficient, the investor is as happy to realize them in Latvia as, say, in Thailand or possibly even western Massachusetts or Connecticut. But the investor will make no sacrifices of his or her own merely in order to better any of these societies. After all, in the contemporary world, one rarely finds large business corporations devoted to the particularistic welfare of the communities within which they have their current plants (which are increasingly mobile if better offers come along from elsewhere). Their loyalties, if any, tend to run far more to their shareholders, who are increasingly drawn from around the world, than to the particular states or even nations within which the present business operations might be located.

Indeed, as already suggested, the rise of the genuinely multinational corporation with genuinely multinational leadership—and multinational lawyers —may itself be a profound commentary on the increasing irrelevance of national citizenship as a meaningful category for most people, especially if we add to this the observation that many corporations put their own cultural stamp on their long-term employees. Even if national citizenship will never become completely irrelevant, one should still contemplate the possibility that it may be taking on the personal meaning that state citizenship has for most of us, i.e., the likely readers of this essay: It might supply us with teams to root for in basketball or soccer tournaments and, more importantly, with a place from which to vote for national political offices or pay taxes in return for public services. It is, though, ever more unlikely to be of any real import in structuring our identities. There is, I suggest, a deep difference between describing oneself as ''coming from North Carolina'' (as I do) or even ''coming from Texas'' (as is the case with my daughters) and ''*being* a North Carolinian or Texan.'' At some point, the same may be true of national background.[25]

Imagine, then, that our non-Latvian investor is faced with a recent law passed by the Latvian parliament that requires a certain kind of expensive antipollution device. The parliament does not seem to have a system of enforcement in place, however, and it is very difficult to detect from surface observation whether the device is being used. Furthermore, the fine imposed, upon discovery, is relatively insubstantial, not more than 5 percent of the cost of the antipollution device. What answer should we expect a lawyer to offer when asked what is Latvian ''law'' on the matter under discussion? Under what legal constraints, that is, must the profit-maximizing corporation operate? More to the point, might the answer to this question differ depending on the nationality of the lawyer? If different lawyers *would* be likely to present different answers, which lawyers—and answers—would we prefer in which contexts, and can the state act to maximize the likelihood of the preferable answers?

The answer to the question about Latvian law would seem to depend on the comparative attention paid by the lawyer to behavior, as against the text found in Latvian lawbooks. It seems clear to me that Latvia would prefer a non-Holmesian (or non-Lukacsian) lawyer and would prefer instead a Kronmanian lawyer imbued with civic values and un-equivocally committed to, and identified with, the welfare of Latvia as presumably defined by the statute requiring the installation of the antipollution device.

How does Latvia (or any other country) get Kronmanian lawyers? One way might be to announce that a central premise of Latvian juris-prudence is that law *is* "law on the books" and that lawyers are to pay no attention to "law in action." This classic bootstrap argument is of no avail. No lawyer actually persuaded by Holmesian jurisprudence and experiencing the material success in society that often attaches, at least in the United States, to its embrace, will be impressed by a statement in the books that law is *not* a prediction of what officials will do or a similar statement mandating that lawyers take account of social values. For what it is worth, *no* state has ever officially promulgated a Holmes-ian definition of law; *all* states pretend that their citizens are bound by the law that can be found in law books. None of this would be particu-larly relevant to a Holmesian lawyer, who would ask whether *that* state-ment, defining law nonpredictively, is likely to have any interesting be-havioral consequences. At this point we are on our way to a classic infinite regress.

Latvia has good reason to doubt that the mere placing of laws on the books would be enough to assure compliance or, more to the point, even attempts by lawyers to assure that their clients would adhere to these laws. Is there *anything* that it might do to increase compliance levels, beyond issuing naive pleas for voluntary obedience or engaging in the costly hiring of more enforcement authorities? Perhaps Latvia would try to maximize the number of Kronmanian "statesman-law-yers" by assuring that lawyers are in fact members of the Latvian state, who presumably identify with its flourishing. Latvia hopes that this will offer at least some protection against the swamping of the legal system by lawyers who view themselves as simply the agents of their clients who are completely private-regarding and may well lack the kinds of ties to Latvia that might otherwise lead to a commitment to its interests.

By adopting a citizenship requirement, then, Latvia is using the for-mal status of citizenship as a proxy for a certain kind of public-regard-ing, communitarian sentiment. Latvian nationals, it might be argued, would be more inclined to steer their clients into respecting the desires—and acting to enhance the welfare—of a newly democratic Latvian state even if that state cannot afford to provide the kind of enforcement mechanisms likely to guarantee desired behavior from the bad man who cares only about the costs of given behavior. Does this make sense for Latvia or for the United States? We come, finally, to the specifics of *In re* Griffiths and its rejection, at least within the American context, of such a limitation.

On *In re* Griffiths

Fre Le Poole Griffiths, who enjoyed the legal status within the United States of a resident alien, was a citizen of the Netherlands who had married someone then teaching at the Yale Law School. She attended an American law school and then applied, in 1970, to take the Connecticut bar examination. After being refused permission to sit for the bar because of her status as a noncitizen, she sued.

On June 25, 1973, two cases were decided by the Supreme Court, both involving the rights of states to restrict certain kinds of positions to citizens. In *Sugarman v Dougall*[26] the Court, through Justice Harry Blackmun, struck down as violative of the Equal Protection Clause of the Fourteenth Amendment a New York law limiting entry into its civil service to United States citizens. Only one—then-Justice Rehnquist—dissented. Ms. Griffiths's case was similarly disposed of, in a quite brief opinion written by Justice Lewis Powell.

Normally the chief justice would have assigned the same justice to write opinions in such similar cases. Justice Blackmun had, indeed, written an earlier opinion dealing with the rights of resident aliens,[27] which easily explains his assignment to write *Sugarman*. What explains the assignment of Powell to write *Griffiths*, I suspect, is the fact that he had been, before being named to the Court in 1971, president of the American Bar Association.[28] Who was better suited, institutionally, to explaining to Connecticut and to the onlooking bar, why states violated the Constitution in limiting membership in the bar to citizens?

Justice Powell noted that membership in the bar had not traditionally been limited to citizens. Ironically enough, his major source for this was an 1873 decision, *Bradwell v Illinois*,[29] (in)famous primarily because it upheld Illinois's refusal to admit Myra Bradwell to the bar solely because she was female. Along the way, however, the earlier Court noted that admission to the bar ''in no sense depends on citizenship of the United States. . . . Certainly many prominent and distinguished lawyers have been admitted to practice, both in the State and Federal courts, who were not citizens of the United States or of any State.''[30] Six years after *Bradwell*, though, in 1879, Connecticut limited admission to the bar to citizens, which Justice Powell suggested was the precursor of a host of restrictions adopted throughout the land designed "to impair significantly the efforts of aliens to earn a livelihood in their chosen occupations.''[31] Whether motivated by nativism or simple rent-seeking desires by citizens to limit the number of potential competitors, these nationality-based restrictions were usually upheld against challenge.

Beginning in 1948, however, the Court began striking down such laws.[32] The major breakthrough came in a 1971 case invalidating distinctions between citizens and resident aliens in regard to eligibility for welfare assistance. "Classifications based on alienage," the Court said through Justice Blackmun, "like those based on nationality or race, are inherently suspect and subject to close judicial scrutiny.''[33] As specialists know, such scrutiny imposes a very high burden of proof on the state, and few laws have managed to survive it. The Connecticut law, of course, was not such a survivor.

Connecticut argued, in Justice Powell's words, "that the special role of the lawyer justifies excluding aliens from the practice of law.''[34] As an "officer of the court," the lawyer is allegedly a quasi-public official, from whom the courts and the public have a right to "demand, according to the Connecticut Supreme Court, which had upheld the restriction, [lawyers'] loyalty, confidence and respect" in order to "foster public confidence in the profession and, consequently, the judicial system.''[35] The state bar, again in Justice Powell's words, "contrasts a citizen's undivided allegiance to this country with a resident alien's possible conflict of loyalties. From this, the Committee concludes that a resident alien lawyer might in the exercise of his functions ignore his responsibilities to the courts or even his client in favor of the interest of a foreign power.''[36]

The majority was unpersuaded by such arguments, not least because Connecticut offered no evidence supporting the proposition "that the practice of law offers meaningful opportunities adversely to affect the interests of the United States.''[37] Justice Powell then included the following very interesting footnote:

> Lawyers frequently represent foreign countries and the nationals of such countries in litigation in the courts of the United States, as well as in other matters in this country. In such representation, the duty of the lawyer, subject to his role as an "officer of the court," is to further the interests

of his clients by all lawful means, even when those interests are in conflict with the interests of the United States or of a State. But this representation involves no conflict of interest in the invidious sense. Rather, it casts the lawyer in his honored and traditional role as an authorized but independent agent acting to vindicate the legal rights of a client, whoever it may be. It is conceivable that an alien licensed to practice law in this country could find himself in a position in which he might be called upon to represent his country of citizenship against the United States in circumstances in which there may be a conflict between his obligations to the two countries. In such rare situations, an honorable person, whether an alien or not, would decline the representation.[38]

Connecticut's interest in ensuring the loyalty of its lawyers could be adequately served, suggested Justice Powell, by its requiring members of the bar to take first an ''attorney's oath'' of integrity in the practice of law and then a ''commissioner's oath'' to ''support the constitution of the United States, and the constitution of the state of Connecticut.''[39] Ms. Griffiths had no hesitation in offering both oaths. It is, of course, scarcely clear what such pledges entail, at least in the absence of a strong theory of constitutional interpretation that resolves potentially conflicting visions of constitutional fidelity.[40] Perhaps for this reason, the Court was quick to point out that Connecticut could also ''properly conduct a character investigation'' and ''continuing scrutiny,'' coupled with the prospect of bar discipline, ''in order to vindicate its undoubted interest in high professional standards.''[41]

Chief Justice Burger joined the majority in *Sugarman*, which dealt with the general civil service, but he dissented in *In re* Griffiths, joined by then-Justice Rehnquist. Although Burger hints that he is of at least two minds about the wisdom of the relative disdain for the importance of citizenship revealed by the majority, the primary ground for his dissent is simply the right of a state, in our federal system of government, to adopt a policy whether or not the Supreme Court believes it to be wise. It is, says Burger, ''reasonable . . . for a State to conclude that persons owing first loyalty to this country will grasp'' its ''traditions and apply our concepts more than those who seek the benefits of American citizenship [such as the right to practice law] while declining to accept the burdens of citizenship in this country.''[42] Obviously, Burger must believe that being a lawyer is significantly different from being an ordinary state bureaucrat and that the state can, in effect, express more concern about who becomes the former than who becomes the latter.

The Canadian Supreme Court, when faced with a similar issue, came to the same decision as did the majority of the United States Supreme

Court, though also over vigorous dissent. A Canadian trial judge had
upheld the limitation of membership in the bar to Canadian citizens,
arguing that "citizenship [is] a personal characteristic which is relevant
to the practice of law on account of *the special commitment to the community which citizenship involves* and not merely because the practical
familarity with the country necessary for the occupation can generally
be expected in the case of citizens."[43] On appeal, however, the court
rejected this reasoning. "Only those citizens who are not natural-born
Canadians," said Judge McLachlin,

> can be said to have made a conscious choice to establish themselves here
> permanently and to opt for full participation in the Canadian social proc-
> ess. . . . While no doubt most citizens, natural-born or otherwise, are com-
> mitted to Canadian society, citizenship does not ensure that that is the
> case. Conversely, non-citizens may be deeply committed to our country.
> Moreover, the requirement of commitment to our country is arguably satis-
> fied by the oath of allegiance which lawyers are required to take. An alien
> may swear that oath. In any event an alien may owe allegiance to the
> Crown if he is resident within this country, even if he does not take the
> oath of allegiance.[44]

Judge McLachlin's reasoning was basically accepted by a majority of
the Supreme Court.

Two of the five justices, however, dissented. For them, citizenship
was indeed a rational proxy for "a commitment to the country and to
the fulfillment of the important tasks" carried out by lawyers. "Citizenship requires the taking on of obligations and commitments to the community, difficult sometimes to describe but felt and understood by most
citizens." The dissenters readily conceded that citizenship is neither a
necessary nor sufficient condition to assure the requisite commitment,
but "to abolish the requirement of citizenship on the basis that it would
fail to insure the attainment of its objectives would . . . be akin to abol-
ishing the law against theft, for it has certainly not insured the elimina-
tion of that crime."[45]

Sugarman and *In re* Griffiths were only the first of what became
several cases dealing with the right to limit public employment to citizens. The Supreme Court has, for example, upheld the limitation of
employment to citizens in the case of members of a state police force[46]
or probation officers within the criminal justice system,[47] even as it
struck down laws like Texas's attempt to prohibit resident aliens from
becoming notaries public.[48] The Court has adopted a " 'political function' exception"[49] to the rules announced in *Sugarman* and *In re* Grif-

fiths. This has been invoked in regard "to laws that exclude aliens from positions intimately related to the process of democratic self-governance."[50]

Perhaps the most interesting application of this "political function" test, in regard to the issues raised by this essay, was in *Ambach v Norwich*,[51] which upheld New York's ban as teachers in public school classrooms of "aliens who have not declared their intent to become citizens." Justifying its decision, the Supreme Court described public school teachers as "possessing a high degree of responsibility and discretion in the fulfillment of a basic governmental obligation." Not only do teachers "have direct, day-to-day contact with students [and] exercise unsupervised discretion over them," they also "act as role models, and influence their students about the government and the political process."[52] For all of these reasons, a state may choose to limit public-school teaching, and other similar roles, to full-fledged members of the political community, at least as measured by the formal status of citizenship.

One could, of course, devote an entire essay to the relevance of citizenship to public school teaching. But I find it difficult to distinguish lawyering from school teaching or working in the criminal justice system. Lawyers often exercise a significant degree of discretion in relating to their clients; far more to the point, one might well argue that a central role of lawyers should be to influence their clients in regard to legal obligations. That is, one might desire that the lawyer be something more than the basically amoral or asocial Holmesian predictor and instead adopt a more Kronmanian role, actively remonstrating with the client to adhere to legal duties even if the prospects of enforcement are relatively low. It is also worth mentioning that a patriot-lawyer might also remonstrate with the client, under some circumstances, to *forgo* enjoying certain legal rights because of their impact on important social values, including the general health of the polity. Under this conception, lawyers identifying themselves as committed citizens of the polity and friends of *its* claims as well as the client's, would view their role as including active engagement with clients about the meaning of engaged citizenship.

There is nothing radical about such a conception of the lawyer's rule. The American Bar Association, for example, has indicated that "[a]dvice of a lawyer to his client need not be confined to purely legal considerations. . . . In assisting his client to reach a proper decision, it is often desirable for a lawyer to point out those factors which may lead to a decision that is morally just as well as legally permissible."[53]

It is important to note that there is no reason to believe that the desires of the state are themselves necessarily moral. This calls into question, therefore, the flat prohibition of the organized bar on "counsel[ing] a client to engage . . . in conduct that the lawyer knows is criminal."[54] One need not, therefore, view the lawyer as a thoughtless cheerleader for the law. A good citizen must be willing on occasion not only to forgo one's legal rights, but also, under some circumstances, to defy the law. But this notion of engaged lawyering (or engaged citizenship) is light-years from the lawyer-as-austere-instrument-of-the-client or the citizen as bad man sketched out by Holmes.

The Lawyer as Transmitter of Core Political Values

Let me turn once more to asking what it is that lawyers—or, for that matter, school teachers—do. This time I would like to contrast the conception of the lawyer (or teacher) as simply the possessor of certain *cognitive* skills or bodies of information with a quite different conception that emphasizes the role played by the lawyer (or teacher) as a transmitter of cultural norms and, indeed, as a model of what it might mean to conceive of oneself as a member of the overarching political community. But, of course, it may be that the actuality of felt membership in fact is so weak, when all is said and done, as to make a mockery of the kinds of analyses described above that give great weight to the status of citizenship.

What has come to be called the standard view of the lawyer's role presents an almost remarkably thin conception of political membership, including that formalization of membership called citizenship. Consider, for example, perhaps the most famous articulation of the lawyer's duty of zealous loyalty to a client. Although the author is Lord Henry Brougham, an English lawyer of the early nineteenth century, it can be found in almost any contemporary American examination of professional responsibility:

> An advocate, in the discharge of his duty, knows but one person in all the world, and that person is his client. To save that client by all means and expedients, and at all hazards and costs to other persons, and, amongst them, to himself, is his first and only duty; and in performing this duty he must not regard the alarm, the torments, the destruction which he may bring upon others. Separating the duty of a patriot from that of an advocate, he must go on reckless of consequences, though it should be his unhappy fate to involve his country in confusion.[55]

In that particular instance, he was threatening to defend his client, Queen Caroline, against King George IV's accusations of adultery by revealing the king's secret marriage to a Catholic, which violated the Act of Settlement of 1689. This presumably would have cost George his crown and, more important, have generated a significant political crisis. Lord Brougham's comment is often quoted for its tone of professed indifference to the "torments" and "destruction" that the lawyer might be visiting upon adversaries or, even worse, upon innocent third parties in the course of vigorous advocacy. Such advocacy obviously raises important questions about the morality of the advocate's enterprise, which has generated hostile response at least since Plato's scathing critique of oratory in *The Gorgias.* But I want to focus more on the "separat[ion of] the duty of the patriot from that of the advocate." This seems to suggest that the lawyer can, at some level, cast off the constraints of citizenship (assuming that this is a proxy for "patriotism") when such constraints would interfere with the lawyer's primary duty of zealous commitment to the interests of the client. To be sure, a lawyer is never entitled, at least from the perspective of the those in control of the legal system itself, to act illegally in behalf of a client (though this observation only underscores the importance of having a cogent theory of what constitutes "the law"); but a lawyer is permitted, indeed encouraged, according to a common understanding of the professional role, to assert with vigor any and all nonfrivolous claims that a client might make, regardless of any social cost they might entail.

What ought we think of such a conception of professional responsibility? Is it fair to suggest that our answer will depend, at least in part, on the extent to which we ourselves feel relatively little patriotism or are otherwise suspicious of strong notions of national loyalty? Also important, I suspect, is the extent to which we adopt a strongly individualist view of the world that views institutions, including the nation-state, primarily as threats to individual liberty, identity, or even the possibility of a moral life. It is quite possible, then, that "citizenship" need not carry as one of its meanings any particular feelings of friendship toward the political order. Indeed, that very view characterizes much American political thought. Many of our political forebears were strongly influenced by antistatist versions of eighteenth-century political thought that have survived into our almost twenty-first-century world. It must also be relevant that such a large part of our population was composed of emigrants from other countries and cultures who, by definition, were sufficiently "unencumbered" to find tolerable and even attractive the leaving behind of old loyalties and identities and to move

to what indeed would become a very new world. To be sure, it is difficult to understand American culture without paying attention to aspects
of American nationalism and, some would say, chauvinism. Yet I wonder how much a view that "no one is going to push *us* around" or that
"we're number one" translates into a genuine notion of community
that leads one genuinely to identify with the travails of strangers who
share "only" common membership in our polity.

It seems ever harder in the United States to envision a sense of shared
enterprise and loyalties that might, for example, lead a lawyer, if not to
refuse work from certain clients, then at least to press in conversation
with the client the claims of one's fellow citizens likely to be hurt by
the client's proposed course of activity. One wonders how much this is
increasingly true of Europe as well. Even as Eastern Europe, in particular, daily offers examples of the most virulent forms of nationalism, we
must recall that the diminution of traditional borders—and, therefore,
almost inevitably of identity—continues in Western Europe. As national
barriers fall in the legal as well as other marketplaces, we might well
expect an ever-diminishing concern on the part of many legal profes-
sionals with the consequences of their clients' activities, unless, of
course, it turns out that a lawyer from London will indeed feel sufficiently "European"—and one from Italy sufficiently "Northern"—to
care deeply about the fate of, say, Italy or the Netherlands, respectively.

A Digression on "Residence"

I have been emphasizing the (ir)relevance of formal membership in a
polity, as symbolized by the passport one carries. But, one might argue,
the more relevant inquiry is less legalistic and more empirical. Perhaps
we should focus on the realities of residence rather than the legal formalities of citizenship. One can readily believe that someone who lives
in Latvia (or Texas), regardless of one's formal citizenship, would in
fact be more concerned about Latvian or Texan welfare than a Latvian
or Texan choosing to live elsewhere. The reason for this belief has nothing to do with perhaps implausible sociopsychological assumptions underlying an emphasis on altruism or civil republicanism and everything
to do with what most of us regard as altogether normal incentives to
look after one's own personal interests. After all, should the quality of
life in Latvia or Texas be diminished, through pollution or anything
else, residents themselves, including, of course, the lawyer, will pay the

cost, which might include bad health as well as diminished property values.

Resident lawyers would have every incentive to limit blind commitment to the client's interests if their attainment would in fact be costly to themselves and their families. One assumes that only the most disciplined lawyers will accept without question the imposition of increased risks on their children even if they are all too willing to foist such risks on the children of others. At the very least, one might count on such lawyers to bring to their clients' attention the potential social costs of the policies under discussion, even if one expects the lawyer loyally to go ahead and attempt to attain the clients' desires upon a declaration that they (the clients) are utterly indifferent to the costs and are interested only in maximizing profits.

For better or worse, the United States Supreme Court has invalidated most state attempts to limit bar membership to state residents.[56] I confess my own support of all such invalidations, for the state policies strike me as far more describable as objectionable barriers to entry mounted by a bar monopoly than as public-regarding regulations designed to protect important civil interests. Similarly, no one alive during the 1960s can forget the importance of outside lawyers who were willing to brave the courthouses of the Deep South in the struggle for civil rights and basic justice. Indeed, reference to the pre-reformed Deep South makes one aware as well of the potential costs of a too-quick acceptance of Kronman's elegiac evocation of membership in a common community by client, lawyer, and judge, as well as his emphasis on incremental prudentialism as the keystone to lawyerly statesmanship. There is almost no place in his scheme for the outside troublemaker who views the community as fundamentally flawed and in need of radical transformation.

But this may simply be to recognize that life is complex and policies can never be analyzed outside of the specific contexts from which they spring. It is possible, therefore, that the factors leading me to express at least a modicum of sympathy for the exclusion of noncitizens from the practice of law might lead me to reconsider at least in part my opposition to limitation on the basis of residency.

Conclusion

So where now do I stand in regard to *In re* Griffiths and the limitation of entrance to the legal profession to American nationals? As already suggested, I am now considerably more ambivalent than I was before my trip to Hungary and my encounter with Ms. Jansone and her resistance to the idea of what might be termed a "cosmopolitan" bar. It no longer strikes me as bigoted or unthinkingly tribalistic to desire that those who join the legal profession, and subject themselves to the norms of professional culture, feel also the pull of other loyalties—the most important one, for our purposes, being the constellation of emotions and identifications often linked with citizenship. This being said, I must also say that I do not see in the contemporary United States a culture that takes citizenship sufficiently seriously to justify the distinction that Connecticut wanted to draw. Connecticut's limitation of bar membership to American citizens—interestingly, Connecticut did not seem to care if its lawyers were citizens of Connecticut itself—seems more mean-spirited, not to mention potentially economically protectionist, than expressive of a rich conception of political community.

I see no meaningful way of turning back toward a richer conception, even if one finds it attractive rather than potentially frightening. I am inclined, however, to think that this is far more a statement about life in the contemporary United States than it is a general truth about how societies should conduct themselves. Small, vulnerable societies, concerned to preserve (or restore) a particularistic culture against the perceived threat of being overwhelmed by cultural outsiders, might legitimately reach different conclusions from our own about the attributes deemed desirable in those who would practice law. At bottom, I suppose the question raised by countries like Latvia is whether we respect their desire *not* to become cosmopolitan and "multicultural" enough to allow them, without criticism, to limit such socially complex occupations as lawyering (or school teaching) to their own citizens.

Perhaps Latvia—not to mention its neighbors to the south in the Balkans—simply illustrates the dreadful ambiguity of the Wilsonian focus on national self-determination. After all, that legacy, so central to American politics in the ensuing seventy-five years, seems to emphasize the legitimacy of groups defined by nationality (or ethnicity) gaining political control over given territory and, therefore, being able to use the coercive power of the state to maintain the national identity. As Daniel Patrick Moynihan eloquently notes, there are good reasons to lament aspects of the Wilsonian heritage.[57] Nationalism that is unleavened by liberalism is frightening indeed.[58]

I myself have no wish to live in a political order defined by ethnicity. For me, one of the glories of the United States is that it is *not* a true *nation*-state, but, rather, a political state composed of many nations.

Even if I sometimes think that the American conception of citizenship is too thin, I have no desire to make it *very* thick. I much prefer the integrative and antinationalist developments in Western Europe to the rediscovery of nationalist roots that seems to pervade contemporary Eastern Europe.

Still, one meaning of multiculturalism is a respect for particularistic cultures, including their desire to maintain their distinctiveness in a cosmopolitan world. And a central question posed by multiculturalism is whether those who are not members (or who do not otherwise identify with) a given culture can sufficiently appreciate challenges to it or accept the necessity of certain measures to maintain it. I cannot reject as irrational a belief that citizenship might be the significant marker of commitment in small (and vulnerable) polities that it may not be in larger (and less vulnerable) ones like our own. I am still not at the point of *supporting* the Latvian prohibition of noncitizen lawyers, but, perhaps more important, I can no longer bring myself to condemn it. As Justice Holmes once put it, "General propositions do not decide concrete cases."[59] Whether discussing Connecticut, Canada, or Latvia, one must play close attention to context in determining the relevance of citizenship (or residence) to such social roles as lawyering.

Notes

1. A somewhat different version of this essay was published as "National Loyalty, Communalism, and the Professional Identity of Lawyers," 7 *Yale Journal of Law and the Humanities* 45 (1995). Permission to incorporate this material is gratefully acknowledged.

2. W. St. John Garwood and W. St. John Garwood, Jr. Regents Chair in Law, University of Texas Law School. I am grateful to Philip Bobbitt, Robert Gordon, Cynthia Y. Levinson, and Martha Minow for responses to earlier versions of this essay, as well as to the faculty colloquium at Vanderbilt University School of Law. The editors of the *Yale Journal of Law and the Humanities* made a number of very helpful suggestions. I am particularly grateful, however, to Williams College, and to Gary Jacobsohn especially, for providing me with the occasion to begin thinking through some of the difficult problems raised by the issue of citizenship in the contemporary world.

3. *Baird v State Bar of Arizona,* 401 US 1 (1971).

4. 413 US 717 (1973).

5. Michael Ignatieff, *Blood and Belonging: Journeys into the New Nationalism* (New York: Farrar, Straus, and Giroux, 1994), 168, notes that the attempt by Latvia to restrict citizenship to Latvian-speakers is quite likely an attempt to

disenfranchise those "ethnic Russians [who] are in a majority in Riga, the capital. . . . Ethnic Russians born and brought up in Latvia lose their citizenship in
the new republic unless they learn the rudiments of Latvian." It is clearly possible to have a multilingual society where given citizens speak only one of the
languages, as in Switzerland, Belgium, or Canada, to offer only three examples.
Perhaps the United States should be added to this list, even though it obviously
has no "official" alternatives to its principal language, unlike the three countries mentioned, which are "officially" bi- or multilingual. In any event, would
it be illegitimate for a state within the United States to restrict entrance to the
bar to those who can speak (at least) English? Only if one confidently answers
this question in the affirmative can one simply dismiss the Latvian language
restriction, which may be not only anti-Russian (which is most certainly is), but
also an attempt to assure the maintenance of Latvian as a living language in a
world where its speakers are surrounded (and potentially swamped) by those
proficient in other languages with no desire to learn Latvian. Ignatieff has an
excellent discussion of the language issue in his discussion of Quebec at pp.
143–177.

   6. Charles Fried, "The Lawyer as Friend: The Moral Foundations of the
Lawyer-Client Relation," 85 *Yale Law Journal* 1060 (1976).

   7. To accept any such argument would, among other things, be especially
difficult for any of us who actually teach in law schools; among other things,
we would presumably have to recognize ourselves as *inevitable* collaborators
with evil.

   8. Michael Walzer, *Obligations: Essays on Disobedience, War, and Citizenship* (Cambridge: Harvard Univ. Press, 1970), 113–114. "[T]he alienated residents of the modern state . . . are probably far more numerous than are the
resident aliens," says Walzer, who goes on to say that whatever obligations are
felt by the politically alienated, "these obligations do not involve what the
ancients called political 'friendship' and do not bind him to share the political
purposes or the political destiny of his fellow residents. . . ."

   9. Fried, "The Lawyer as Friend," 1071.

   10. Francis Lieber, 1 Manual of Political Ethics 89 (originally published
1855, 1881 ed.), as quoted in Paul Carrington, "The Theme of Early American
Law Teaching: The Political Ethics of Francis Lieber," 42 *J. Legal Ed* 339, 369
(1992).

   11. For high political theory, see, e.g., Michael Sandel, *Liberalism and the
Limits of Justice* (New York: Cambridge University Press, 1982); for more popular books written by academics, see Mary Ann Glendon, *Rights Talk: The
Impoverishment of Political Discourse* (New York: Free Press, 1991). Robert
Bellah *et al.*, *Habits of the Heart: Individualism and Commitment in American
Life* (New York: Harper & Row, 1986). Even some liberal critics of the new
communitarianism nonetheless recognize the need for individuals to have social
commitments. See, e.g., Nancy Rosenblum, *Another Liberalism: Romanticism
and Reconstruction of Liberal Thought* (Cambridge, Mass.: Harvard University
Press, 1987).

12. See Connecticut General Statutes §1–25 (1987). I discuss the oath in "Suffrage and Community: Who Should Vote?" 41 *Florida Law Review* 545: 560–61 (1989).

13. Anthony T. Kronman, *The Lost Lawyer: Failing Ideas of the Legal Profession* (Cambridge, Mass.: Belknap Press of Harvard University Press, 1993), 93.

14. Steven M. Cohen, *American Modernity and Jewish Identity* (New York: Tavistock Publications, 1983), 84. I explore some of these themes in "Identifying the Jewish Lawyer: Reflections on the Construction of Professional Identity," 14 *Cardozo Law Review* 1577 (1993).

15. See the remarkable essay by Monroe E. Price, "The Market for Loyalties: Electronic Media and the Global Competition for Allegiances," 104 *Yale LJ* 667 (1994), concerning the implications especially for European countries of the loss of control over the radio and television that occupy the airwaves within given political entities.

16. 10 *HarvLRev* 457, 477 (1897).

17. See, e.g., Kronman, *Lost Lawyer*, 134. "When a lawyer gives advice to a client based upon his prediction of the future course of judicial behavior, he is engaged in an enterprise that, broadly speaking, includes the work of judges too, namely the maintenance of the rule of law *in the political society to which lawyer, judge, and client all belong*" (emphasis added).

18. Kronman, *Lost Lawyer*, 145.

19. Robert W. Gordon, "The Independence of Lawyers," *BULRev* 1 (1988). See also Robert W. Gordon, "Corporate Law Practice as a Public Calling," MdLRev 255 (1990).

20. Reich's comments are quoted in Christopher Lasch, "The Revolt of the Elites: Have They Canceled Their Allegiance to America?" *Harper's*, November 1994, 49. Reich is also cited for his fear about the "secession of the symbolic analysts" from membership in the ordinary polity. As one can readily gather from the subtitle of his essay, Lasch, who died earlier this year, was extremely fearful of the consequences of any such secession. One assumes that he would have been extremely sympathetic to Dean Kronman's attempt to revive a more citizenship-oriented conception of lawyering.

21. Georg Lukacs, *History and Class Consciousness: Studies in Marxist Dialectics* (Cambridge, Mass.: MIT Press, 1971), 263.

22. See, e.g., Kimberly Garcia, "Office wagering not quite so risky," *Austin American-Statesman* (23 January 1993), B1 (about office Super Bowl pools and unlikelihood of enforcement of the law prohibiting them).

23. See, e.g., Stuart Taylor, Jr, "Inside the Whirlwind: How Zoë Baird Was Monstrously Caricatured For the Smallest of Sins, Pounded by Press and Popular Righteousness, and Crucified by Prejudice and Hypocrisy," *The American Lawyer* (March 1993): 64–69. The matter of social security taxes is more complex, although there seems to be good evidence that Ms. Baird and her husband were in fact the victims of bad legal advice rather than conscious evaders of

their legal duties. In any event, even after the widespread publicity about Ms. Baird, it is unlikely in the extreme that most Americans are now paying social security taxes for every teenager who has been paid more than $50 in a calendar quarter to baby-sit or mow the lawn, although it is probably true that many of those who contemplate future public office may be changing their behavior on this matter.

24. Perhaps I should note at this point that I know almost nothing about the actual system of Latvian law. I assume that, like all Continental legal systems, it is code oriented rather than a common-law system. It may also be the case that fifty years of Soviet hegemony within Latvia left lawyers within that country with significantly different conceptions of their role than would have been the case had the Nazi-Soviet Pact of 1939—which allowed the Soviet Union its unchallenged takeover of the Baltic states—not occurred. The discussion in the text concerns the general theoretical problem of the right of a state to attempt to control the ideological structure of the legal profession. To the extent that specific facts matter, I exercise the prerogative of law professors to stipulate them when convenient for my argument.

25. Indeed, the word ''background'' is interesting in this context, for one way of defining this inquiry is establishing the conditions under which one's citizenship status will be ''foregrounded,'' either by the state or, perhaps more significantly, by a lawyer herself.

26. 413 US 634 (1973).

27. See *Graham v Richardson*, 403 US 365 (1971).

28. See John Jeffries, *Lewis Powell* (New York: Scribner's/Macmillin Pub., 1994), 194–104, 210–11.

29. 83 US (16 Wall.) 130 (1873).

30. 83 US (16 Wall.) 139 (1873), quoted at 413 U S 719. Indeed, it may also be worth noting that many states at this time allowed at least some resident aliens to vote, even in elections for national office—a practice that ended in the United States only in 1928.

31. 413 US 719 (1973).

32. See *Takahashi v Fish & Game Commission*, 334 US 410 (1948).

33. *Graham v Richardson*, 403 US 365, 372 (1971).

34. 403 US 723 (1971).

35. 162 Conn. 249, 262–63, 294 A.2d 281, 287 (1972).

36. 413 US 724 (1973).

37. 413 US 724 (1973).

38. 413 US 724 n. 14 (1973).

39. 413 US 725–26 (1973).

40. I have explored such questions in Sanford Levinson, *Constitutional Faith* (Princeton, N.J.: Princeton University Press, 1988), chapters 3 and 4.

41. 413 US at 726–27 (1973).

42. 413 US 733 (1973).

43. See *Andrews v Law Society of British Columbia*, 22 DLR (4th) 9, 21

(1986), quoted in *Andrews v Law Society of British Columbia*, 56 DLR (4th) 1, 35 (1989). (Emphasis added.) I am grateful to Lorraine Weinrib and Alex Aleinikoff, who informed me of the existence of *Andrews* and its obvious relevance to my project.

44. 27 DLR (4th) 600, 612–13 (1986), quoted at 56 DFR (4th) 43.

45. See 56 DLR (4th) 29 (opinion of Justice McIntyre).

46. *Foley v Connelie*, 435 US 291 (1978).

47. *Cabell v Chavey-Salido*, 454 US 432 (1982).

48. *Bernal v Fainter*, 467 US 216 (1984).

49. 467 US 220 (1984).

50. 467 US 220 (1984).

51. 441 US 68 (1979).

52. 467 US 220 (1984).

53. American Bar Association, *Model Code of Professional Responsibility and Code of Judicial Conduct* (Chicago: American Bar Association, 1978), E[thical] C[onsideration] 7–8. See also American Bar Association, Model Rules of Professional Conduct (Chicago: American Bar Association, 1983), 2.1: "In rendering advice, a lawyer may refer not only to law but to other considerations such as moral, economic, social and political factors, that may be relevant to the client's situation." I can testify that few law students seem to find such a potential role as moral counselor attractive or even plausible. Most view any such role as an incursion on the autonomy of the client, who is presumed either to have thought through in advance any moral or political dilemmas or to be impervious to the lawyer's own potential suggestions. Full analysis of the actual impact of the American Bar Association's delineation of the lawyer's role is far beyond the scope of this essay.

54. American Bar Association, *Model Rules of Professional Conduct*, 1.2(b).

55. As quoted in David Luban, *Lawyers and Justice: An Ethical Study* (Princeton, N.J.: Princeton University Press, 1988), 54–55. Luban's book, incidentally, is obviously relevant to the general issues presented in this essay, especially insofar as he offers a vigorous critique of Holmesian lawyering at 20–30. I focus on Dean Kronman's book, however, because it is more self-consciously written within the civic republican critique of the kind of egoistic liberalism linked with Holmes.

56. See, e.g., *Barnard v Thorstenn*, 489 US 546 (1989); *District of Columbia Court of Appeals v Feldman*, 460 US 462 (1983).

57. See Daniel Patrick Moynihan, *Pandaemonium: Ethnicity in International Politics* (Oxford, England, and New York: Oxford University Press, 1993), especially chapter 2, "On the 'Self-Determination of Peoples,'" 63–106.

58. See Yael Tamir, *Liberal Nationalism* (Princeton, N.J.: Princeton University Press, 1993).

59. *Lochner v New York*, 198 US 45, 76 (1905).

3

Nationhood and Citizenship:
What Difference Did the American
Revolution Make?

by Pauline Maier

On May 10, 1776, the Massachusetts General Court asked the inhabitants of each town within the Commonwealth to debate the following question ''in full Meeting warned for that Purpose'': should the honourable Continental Congress, for the safety of the Colonies, declare them independent of Great Britain, would they ''solemnly engage'' to defend that decision with their lives and fortunes?[1]

It was more than a year since the war with Britain had begun at Lexington Green, and almost two months since cannon dragged from Ticonderoga to Dorchester Heights had helped force the British to evacuate Boston. The next phase of the war, in New York, had not yet begun. In the meantime, the Second Continental Congress—which had first convened on May 10, 1775, exactly one year before the General Court's vote—was moving slowly and not so surely toward affirming American independence. The main obstacle was a block of Middle Colonies, particularly New York, Pennsylvania, and Maryland, that in late 1775 had instructed their congressional delegates against voting for independence, and never saw fit to withdraw those instructions. Members of the Massachusetts delegation thought that if the Bay Colony stated ''with decent Firmness'' its support for independence, its example might ''turn many doubtful Minds, and produce a Reversion of the contrary Instructions adopted by some Assemblies.''[2] But the General Court's effort to build a grass roots movement within the Bay Colony foundered. The towns were supposed to instruct their newly elected assembly representatives to favor independence, but internal political maneuvering and communications difficulties meant that they debated independence at meetings held in May, June, and on into July, well after the new assembly first met. It was therefore not a Massachusetts delegate, but Virginia's Richard Henry Lee who, acting on recent instructions from his home colony, on 7 June 1776 moved in Congress

> That these United Colonies are, and of right ought to be, free and independent States, that they are absolved from all allegiance to the British Crown, and that all political connection between them and the State of Great Britain is, and ought to be, totally dissolved.[3]

The votes of Massachusetts's towns remain fascinating nonetheless. They took on the task assigned them with an occasional expression of awe from town fathers more accustomed to addressing the perennial problems of wandering hogs and fallen fences: this, commented Topsfield on 21 June, is "the greatest and most important question that ever came before this town." The issue warranted seriousness; to commit one's life and fortune to the cause was to face straight on the punishment given traitors—death and the confiscation of estate. At least one town, Barnstable on Cape Cod, decided in the negative, though it later explained that it had intended only to let its legislative representative decide how to vote on the issue.[4] Other towns voted yes, sometimes explaining their decisions, sometimes not. But even the briefest statements of commitment often had an eloquence that, to my ear, compares well with the more familiar and sometimes labored prose of the Declaration of Independence Thomas Jefferson drafted for the Continental Congress. Take, for example, the town of Ashby, a small farming community near the New Hampshire border. Like other towns, it carefully rephrased the assembly's request when it unanimously voted on July 1 that, should

> the honourable Congress, for the safety of the Colonies, declare them independent of Great Britain, the inhabitants of Ashby will solemnly engage with their lives and fortunes to support them in the measures.

Or consider the resolution of Greenwich, a town whose ghostly remains, I have been told, can be seen on a clear day beneath the surface of the Quabbin Reservoir. At a legal town meeting held in a public house, the townsmen

> Voted for independence on *Great Britain* if the honourable *American* Congress thinks fit, and most for the interest of the Colonies; it being a unanimous vote,

and, if that wasn't clear enough, added for good measure "not one dissenting."[5]

What relevance do these events carry for citizenship and nationhood, the subjects of these essays? With regard to the United States, those topics can be addressed only because of changes that came with the American Revolution. Before 1776, there were no American "citizens," only American "subjects" of George III; there was no nation, only a set of British North American colonies that had no link with each other except through the British government. We want to know more, of course: we want to know what difference it made for colonies to become a nation, for subjects to become citizens. Witnesses as we are to the problems of nation-building or rebuilding in Eastern Europe, we also want to know what allowed Americans to create one nation out of what could have been many, a nation in which ethnic and religious particularisms were subsumed into a larger whole. The union formed in the eighteenth century was, of course, imperfect, or the Civil War would not have happened. And yet, against the example of Ireland, for example, or what was Yugoslavia, the American creation of one from many—e pluribus unum—remains striking. In exploring that subject, it is important to understand that the words "nation" and "citizen" have changed in meaning over time.[6] Because I propose to concentrate on the beginnings of American nationhood and citizenship, it makes some sense to go back to the testimony of those who took part in the decision for independence.

In truth, today virtually all statements on the meaning of the American nation cite Congress's Declaration of Independence. Or, more exactly, its assertion that "all men are created equal" and are "endowed by their Creator with certain unalienable rights" among which are "life, liberty, and the pursuit of happiness"—words wrenched from their context in the document and separated from the critical conclusions Jefferson drew from them. Take note of the constant reference to the Declaration and also the Constitution: it suggests the centripetal role that documents, and the ideals associated with them—equality, rights, popular sovereignty, limited power, rule of law—have played in the United States, providing the foundation for a consensus that has served to cut across and mitigate profound social and political differences. How else can we explain the extraordinary efforts taken to preserve our nation's vital documents? Encased since 1952 "in bronze-framed glass containers filled with helium and water vapor," the Declaration of Independence and Constitution were recently examined at the National Archives for evidence of degeneration by conservators using the most advanced technological processes, including a $3.3 million Charters Monitoring System specially developed for that purpose. Conservators scrutinized them with a fiber-optic light source, scanned them section by section with a computer imaging process capable of observing tiny flecks of eighteenth-century ink, and carefully mapped each crease or glue spot, each tear or minute imperfection on their parchment base— all in an effort to preserve for future generations those "visible symbols" of our nation and its revolutionary origins. Those founding documents have become for the United States what Lenin's body was for the Soviet Union.[7]

As an expression of the convictions that lay behind the creation of a nation from colonies, of citizens from subjects, Jefferson's Declaration of Independence was but one among many, most of which have been forgotten. Of particular interest here are what I call the "other declarations of independence"—the formal declarations of independence from Britain that some states issued in the spring and summer of 1776, the often equally elaborate documents adopted by the revolutionary congresses, conventions, or conferences of such other states as Pennsylvania instructing their congressional delegates to vote for independence, and similar statements on that issue from such local groups as New York City's "General Committee of the Mechanics in Union" or from more broadly representative local bodies including county meetings in Maryland and Virginia, grand juries in South Carolina, and, of course, Massachusetts towns.[8] Such documents have a feeling of authenticity to them. They seem to state directly and without contrivance the convictions of the people, and they probably did so in the case of the resolutions of Massachusetts towns, or of James City County, Virginia, which were signed by a majority of the freeholders. In general, however, the surviving local resolutions and declarations on independence were the work of only a part of the American people—those politically active white men in communities that, for reasons stemming from the peculiarities of contemporary politics, were moved to announce and often also to explain their support for independence between April and July 1776. They nonetheless suggest much about the origins and character of American nationhood and citizenship.

Start with nationhood. The several declarations of independence testify, first of all, to the reluctance with which the colonists accepted their destiny as an independent nation, an attitude that sets revolutionary Americans apart from modern nationalists. "A few years, ago, sir," said the townsmen of Topsfield, the question whether or not they were ready to commit their lives and fortunes to American independence

> would have put us in a surprise, and we apprehend, would have been treated with the utmost contempt. We then looked on ourselves happy in being subjects of the King of *Great Britain*. It being our forefathers' native country, we looked up unto them as our parent state; and we have always looked upon it as our duty, as well as our interest, to defend and support the honour of the Crown of *Great Britain*, and we have always freely done it, both with our lives and fortunes—counting ourselves happy when in the strictest union and connection with our parent State. But the scene is now changed; our sentiments are now altered.[9]

What caused so profound an alteration of sentiment? To explain was important for a people who agreed, in Jefferson's words, that "governments long established should not be changed for light & transient causes." Topsfield asserted that "she who was called our mother country and parent State" had become the colonies' "greatest enemy." It referred to "unprovoked injuries," to "unjustifiable and unconstitutional claims" enforced in ways that were "cruel and unjust to the highest degree," to objectionable conduct by the "Court of *Great Britain*" and its governors that were "so well known" and had been "by much abler hands, set forth in such a clear, plain, and true light," that it was "needless to enumerate any further particulars."[10]

Others, particularly provincial congresses and conventions, took the trouble to enumerate the causes of independence in greater detail. In most cases they concentrated upon a set of charges stemming from well-known events of 1775 and 1776. They complained that the king had "paid no regard" to the colonists' "numerous and dutiful petitions" for reconciliation and a redress of grievances, answering even the Continental Congress's carefully drafted, respectful "Olive Branch" petition of July 1775 with "increased insult, oppression, and a vigorous attempt to effect our total destruction"; that he had formally put the colonists out of his protection by consenting to the infamous Prohibitory Act of December 1775 that made American vessels and their cargoes forfeit to the Crown as if they were the property of open enemies; that his servants had "excited the savages of this country to carry on a war against us, as also the negroes to imbrue their hands in the blood of their masters, in a manner unpracticed by civilized nations," burned American towns such as Falmouth, Maine, and Norfolk, Virginia; and, finally, that the king had negotiated treaties with various German states to purchase "foreign troops to assist in enslaving us." These events made it absurd for the colonists to profess continued allegiance to George III: they left the colonists "no alternative . . . but an abject submission . . . or a total separation from the Crown and Government of *Great Britain.*" Compelling reasons founded on justice, policy, and simple necessity argued for "a radical separation from *Great Britain.*" Indeed, because "the obligations of allegiance" were "reciprocal," the "despotism" of the king, as Pennsylvania put it, dissolved the colonists' obligations to him. The town of Alford in Berkshire County drew the same conclusion: Britain had itself sundered the "connection between *Great Britain* and the United Colonies of *North America*" and made America independent. That fate was emphatically not the colonists' choice. Even after formally declaring their and their constituents' "willingness to concur in a vote of the Congress declaring the United Colonies free and independent States" on 24 June the Pennsylvania provincial conference insisted that their declaration "did not originate in ambition, or in an impatience of lawful authority, but that we were driven to it . . . by the oppressions and cruelties of the aforesaid King and Parliament of *Great Britain.*"[11]

As explanations or justifications of independence, these provincial and local documents are, I think, more effective than Congress's Declaration of Independence, which proposed to tell mankind why it had become necessary "for one people to dissolve the political bands which have connected them with another, and to assume among the powers of the earth" a "separate and equal station." Jefferson included a long and often vague list of charges against George III, many of which remain difficult even for historians to associate with identifiable events. When exactly during the colonists' conflict with Britain did the king refuse his assent to laws "the most wholesome and necessary for the public good," call together legislatures "at places unusual, uncomfortable, & distant from . . . their public records," or endeavor "to prevent the population of these States"? Could anyone argue that such events were critical in the colonists' painful move from subjects to citizens between 1775 and 1776?[12]

More important, together these documents testify to a second significant point: the American nation was born of revolution. Jefferson's well-remembered statement that all men were created equal with unalienable rights opened a powerful assertion of the right of revolution—a right that was of critical importance in 1776. To secure those inalienable rights, he went on, "governments are instituted among men, deriving their just powers from the consent of the governed," and so "whenever any form of government becomes destructive of these ends, it is the right of the people to alter or to abolish it, and to institute new government. . . ." Even the document's attribution of grievances to the king signaled its revolutionary character. In English law and tradition, injustices were customarily attributed to the king's ministers until they became so serious as to dissolve the legitimacy of the state. At that point the king himself, as the repository of sovereignty, was made responsible: in this Americans of 1776 followed a long-established English precedent, one observable, among other examples, in the Declaration of Rights issued by England's convention parliament of 1689.[13]

The eloquent declarations of local bodies suggest that outrage at British actions was widespread; indeed, by modern estimates, Loyalists represented only about 20 percent of the population and were scattered individually or in small pockets over extensive territory. The existence of a common outside enemy and the dangerousness of a situation in which the British were waging open war on the colonists and in which British policy repeatedly attempted to separate some colonies from the others served to make American unity essential. As the Associators of Anne Arundel County put it on June 22, 1776, "the true interests and substantial happiness of the United Colonies in general, and this in particular," were "inseparable interwoven and linked together, and essentially dependent upon a close Union and Continental Confederation. . . . By division, the most diabolical wishes of the King, Lords, and Commons, will be effectually realized."[14] Harmony would prove more difficult to sustain in peacetime. Still, the wartime origins of the American state provided an important precedent as well as a shared tradition that bound the various states together in a nation they would continue until after the Civil War to call "the Union," suggesting its nature as a whole constructed of distinct parts.

The various declarations of independence suggest, finally, how essential the creation of new governments was to the cause of revolution. By the spring of 1776 many Americans were convinced that their problems were rooted not in the malevolence of individuals but, as Thomas Paine asserted in *Common Sense*, in the system of monarchy and hereditary rule. In fact, in December 1775, before Paine's pamphlet was published, the radical revolutionaries of Pittsfield described the nomination and appointment of provincial officials by the king a "secret poison" that lay behind "all the Evils & Calamities" that had befallen both Massachusetts and the United Colonies. The draft constitution that Thomas

Jefferson wrote for Virginia in May or June 1776 carefully and explicitly linked the king's failures with an abandonment of monarchy.
After listing the colonies' grievances and declaring that by those ''acts
of misrule'' George III had ''forfeited the kingly office,'' Jefferson
called for the abolition of kingship, ''which all experience hath shown
inimical'' to public liberty. ''Be it therefore enacted by the authority of
the people,'' Jefferson's draft went on, that George III

> hereby is deposed from the kingly office within this government and abso-
> lutely divested of all it's [sic] rights, powers and prerogatives; and that he
> and his descendants and all persons claiming by or through him, and all
> other persons whatsoever shall be & for ever remain incapable of the same;
> and that the said office shall henceforth cease and never more either in
> name or substance be re-established within this colony.

At about the same time the people of Pittsfield, Massachusetts, instructed their representative to the General Court (a man with the engaging name of Valentine Rathbun) to use his influence so Massachusetts would notify the Continental Congress ''that this whole Province
are waiting for the important moment which they in their great wisdom
shall appoint for the declaration of Independence and *a free Repub-
lick.*''[15]

The statements of contemporaries strongly suggest that for them the
word ''republic'' implied first and foremost a form of government, one
without monarchy or hereditary rule, in which all power came from
popular consent. The adoption of republican government was built upon
a powerful sense of popular empowerment that emerged in the course
of the struggle with Britain. Consider the argument for independence
that Natick, Massachusetts, offered on 20 June 1776: the townsmen of
Natick had become converted to independence, they said, not only by
the ''unenlightened and uncivilized'' actions of Britain, but by

> the glaring impropriety, incapacity, and fatal tendency, of any State what-
> ever, at the distance of three thousand miles, to legislate for these Colo-
> nies, which at the same time are so numerous, so knowing, and capable of
> legislating. . . .

In other words, they had come to realize almost by surprise that Americans could govern themselves more effectively. Six months earlier the
precocious people of Pittsfield put it in a more provocative way. Unless
the right of nominating officers was invested in the people, they said,

they were "indifferent who assumes it whether . . . on this or the other side of the [w]ater."[16]

The testimony of one revolutionary spokesman after another contradicts the effort of modern scholars to make of the American Revolution something other than a movement whose revolutionary character was founded upon the political and institutional transformations it brought.[17] Distressed because he was stuck at Congress in May 1776 when he wanted desperately to be in Williamsburg, participating in the convention that would draft Virginia's new state constitution, Thomas Jefferson wrote that the institution of a government better than that of the past was the "whole object of the present controversy." Suggestions of the enthusiasm with which that task was undertaken lie in the care with which states, while affirming independence, reserved to themselves power over forming the new governments for their people, and also in the delight expressed by the grand jurymen of the Cheraws District in north central South Carolina in May 1776 at the new, popular-based government already established in that state. Their conclusion that the change of government "every one once dreaded as the greatest misery, they now unexpectedly find their greatest advantage." The jury then movingly recommended

> to every man . . . to secure and defend with his life and fortune a form of Government so just, so equitable, and promising; to inculcate its principles to their children, and hand it down to them unviolated, that the latest posterity may enjoy the virtuous fruits of that work, which the integrity and fortitude of the present age had, at the expense of their blood at treasure, at length happily effected.[18]

The problem remained how best to construct modern "republican" governments, and that challenge fascinated relatively obscure Massachusetts townsmen no less than the likes of John Adams, who celebrated the fact that he lived in an age in which the greatest lawgivers of the ancient world would have chosen to live. Having been consulted on independence, the towns later debated the merits of state constitutions proposed for their approval in 1778 and 1780 (and, later, the federal Constitution of 1787). On the insistence of "Constitutionalists" in Pittsfield and other rural towns, a special convention of elected delegates—not the state legislature—drafted Massachusetts's constitution of 1780, which was then submitted to the towns for direct popular ratification. The constitution became therefore a direct act of legislation by the people and the first revolutionary state constitution to proclaim that

"We . . . the people of Massachusetts . . . DO agree upon, ordain and establish, the following *Declaration of Rights*, and *Frame of Government*, as the CONSTITUTION OF THE COMMONWEALTH OF MASSACHUSETTS."[19]

The Philadelphia Convention of 1787 borrowed that phrase, beginning its proposed constitution with a statement that "We the people of the United States . . . do ordain and establish this Constitution for the United States of America." By building the government of the nation on popular ratification through state constitutional conventions, not legislative consent, the Founders established, as they came to understand in the course of the ratification debates, a modern federal system. In the United States, both state and national governments exercised defined and limited powers that had been granted directly by the sovereign people. National government under the new Constitution was not the creation of the states' governments, as the Confederation had been. Instead state and nation were siblings, parts of a single political family, each with different and complementary powers. American federalism was a masterpiece of eighteenth-century political engineering, a means of combining communities with distinctive cultures, traditions, and interests in a larger whole, of creating one out of many.

The American nation was, then, born reluctantly in the midst of a revolution that empowered the people, released a surge of excitement for a republicanism that was essentially governmental, and produced a novel federal system that served to reconcile national community with regional particularism. What implications did that achievement have for citizenship?

It stands to reason that in a republic, where all authority comes from the people, the character of the nation and that of its citizens are necessarily closely bound. That insight shaped a substantial body of scholarship over the past twenty years. American eighteenth-century ideas of republican citizenry, we were told, drew on the example of the ancients as it was passed to more modern political theorists through the writings of Machiavelli. Republics were supposedly by nature turbulent and ephemeral. The formidable challenge of founding a stable republic demanded the creation of a virtuous citizenry, one willing to sacrifice private pleasures for the public welfare, as in Sparta, the most stable of the ancient republics. Efforts to establish such a civic humanist or classical republican society warred against commerce and the emergent institutions of modern capitalism and had to give way, as the story went, before a modern liberal state could emerge.

More recent scholarship has happily discredited or severely modified that argument. Surely Americans of the late eighteenth century saw themselves as part of a republican lineage that reached back to the ancient world: think of the statues of George Washington or Benjamin Franklin dressed somewhat incongruously in togas, of the revival of the word "Senate," of the earnest statements by one revolutionary leader after another that virtue was essential for the republic's survival. But, according to Paul Rahe's monumental *Republics, Ancient and Modern: Classical Republicanism and the American Revolution* (1992), Americans soon came to understand how fundamentally different their republic would necessarily be from its ancient predecessors.[20] One difference lay in the extent and social character of its citizenry.

Who qualified as citizens of the United States at the end of the eighteenth century? Here, let us admit, we embark on a subject of forbidding complexity. As late as 1862 the attorney general of the United States confessed that he had long and fruitlessly searched law books and court records

> for a clear and satisfactory definition of the phrase *citizen of the United States*. . . . Eighty years of practical enjoyment of citizenship, under the Constitution, have not sufficed to teach us either the exact meaning of the word, or the constitutional elements of the thing we prize so highly.[21]

Less exactly, however, the terms "citizens" and even "the people" of the United States in an eighteenth-century sense referred to members of the polis or political community, those who could vote and hold office, all of whom were adult white men. They did not, however, defend their interests alone, as male heads of households were assumed also to speak for the women, children, and servants or slaves in their families.

There were, of course, anomalies, such as single women, who were clearly members of the community and sometimes also tax-paying property holders, but who had no enfranchised husband to speak for them and thus could not vote themselves. There also were free blacks, of whom there were very few in the United States at the time of independence, but whose numbers multiplied over the next quarter century for reasons tied to the transformation of Americans from subjects to citizens. The equality of the early republic meant, if nothing else, that no man was born subject to another. That understanding of equality was intimately tied to the abolition of hereditary rule, which was itself essential to American republicanism. Slavery constituted an obvious anomaly in a modern republic as slaves were born subject to others.

Moreover, the hypocrisy of slaveholders' protesting their enslavement did not go unnoticed. One result was a wave of emancipation after independence that gradually eliminated slavery in the Northern states. The South was more hesitant, but in the upper states of the region for at least a brief period legislatures facilitated private emancipations. The question soon arose whether the freed blacks were citizens of the United States. It was not readily answered; indeed, that issue prompted the attorney general's expression of puzzlement in 1862, and was only definitively resolved in 1868 with the Fourteenth Amendment.

Accustomed as we are to emphasizing the continuing problems of gender and race, we are inclined to emphasize the restrictions on early republican citizenship. But against the example of the ancient world, where civic participation was limited to an elite, or, indeed, compared to any other nation of the time, American citizenship was extraordinarily comprehensive and has evolved over time toward greater inclusiveness. Property qualifications for the vote or for office holding imposed by the first state constitution gave way in the federal Constitution to less restrictive requirements of age and residency, then gradually disappeared in the states as their original constitutions were replaced or revised. Efforts to impose enduring political disabilities on persons of non-American origin failed: the nationalization acts of the 1790s allowed immigrants to become full-fledged citizens, equal with the native born, after a defined period of residency. Even religious differences—which caused perhaps the most acute sociopolitical conflicts of mid-eighteenth-century America—gradually ceased to carry civil disabilities. So widespread did political rights become that to be denied them became invidious. Consider the protest of Philadelphia Jews against a provision in Pennsylvania's 1776 constitution that required assembly delegates to affirm that both the old and new testaments were of divine origin. That requirement, a Jewish spokesman argued, contradicted a provision in the state's bill of rights that said no man who acknowledged the existence of God could be "deprived or abridged of any civil right." In truth, he acknowledged, the Jews weren't "perticulary" anxious to sit in the assembly, but to be deprived of that opportunity imposed a "stigma upon their nation and religion."[22] Soon blacks and women would also find a similar argument for enfranchisement in documents adopted at the time of the Revolution: the equality asserted at first, before governments were founded, as the state of men in the state of nature became in the hands of blacks and women a principle of civil society that warred against all obstacles to full participation in the rights and privileges of citizenship.

A relatively extensive citizenry was only one attribute that distinguished the American republic from its predecessors. The ancient republics were essentially militaristic; and that most admired in the eighteenth century, Sparta, intensified public commitment by eliminating the distractions of family and commerce and giving little heed to the arts or technology. But the attempt under the federal Militia Act of 1792 to require militia service of all white males between the ages of 18 and 45 failed miserably. Americans were not just suspicious of armies, but powerfully committed to family, enthusiastic for commerce, and delighted with improvements that made life easier or more profitable.

From those characteristics emerged perhaps the most peculiar device for harnessing private effort to the public welfare—for institutionalizing virtue in a commercial republic, if you will: the corporation. In contemporary Europe corporations were considered unenlightened repositories of privilege; yet, beginning in the 1780s, American legislatures—led by that of Massachusetts—reformed and adapted them to its needs and created so many that, by 1830, there were said to be more corporations, especially of the profit-making sort, in the United States than in any other nation.[23]

We tend to look at these early-day corporations as the ancestors of IBM, which they were; but in the late eighteenth and early nineteenth centuries they remained modest affairs, made up of a limited number of people associated together to serve—and this was a critical requirement—some public good. Chartered groups received a legal identity, the right to own and manage property and to protect their assets in the courts as well as limited powers of self-government. Essentially the corporation provided a means by which the states could enlist private capital and energies to promote projects for the public's benefit. Corporations were created to build bridges, roads, and similar public improvements; for banks and manufactories, religious societies and charities, and, of particular interest here, schools and colleges.

Educational corporations were surely among the most important of the early republic. The revolution all but mandated the establishment of a more extensive educational system to educate voters and also to allow the community to draw upon the talents of all its people, and so to distinguish it from the Old World where the monopolization of knowledge by the few allowed them to tyrannize a "despised, enslaved, and stupid multitude." Elaborate schemes for public school systems were proposed, but rarely came to fruition; instead the age saw a flowering of private academies and colleges, often founded under state charters of incorporation.[24]

The chartering of Williams College in 1793—an event that would not have occurred without the Revolution's release of a new hostility toward privilege, including the monopolistic status of Harvard College—is in many ways characteristic of that movement. The Williams charter reflected the period of its origin in the powers it granted and the limits imposed on them and in its explicit understanding that the college would promote virtue, piety, and knowledge—a cause so closely bound to the interest of the state that the legislature contributed funds for its support "out of the treasure of the Commonwealth." The trustees' petition requesting incorporation promised that Williams would bring liberal education "more within the power of the middling and lower classes of citizens" (a nontraditional ambition if ever there was one), to extend the culture and improve the manners of young men from the neighboring states of Vermont, New York, and Connecticut for fees that would "add to the influence and wealth of Massachusetts," and to contribute to the "lustre and renown" of a state they prayed might become "the Athens of the United States of America."[25] Can one imagine a more productive effort to harness the particularism of state loyalty to the benefit of a larger public good? Or a more selective choice of a model from antiquity, one that referred to Athens as the home of learning in pleading for an educational mission whose professed purposes were at odds with the narrow constraints of traditional elitism? In the professed purposes of Williams' founders we glimpse, then, how the Revolution not only founded a nation, but began to shape its character.

The strength of the new nation clearly depended upon the support of its constituent parts—towns, counties, states—and upon the republic's capacity to inspire and sustain groups of citizens willing to undertake projects of use to the public as well as themselves. And in time, the nation grew by multiplying the "many" from which the "one" had been constructed: it absorbed new states which became equals of the old, and new peoples who assumed rights and responsibilities identical to those of the native-born. The process was, of course, never easy, or the outcome free of doubt, even after Appomattox. The result, however, was a nation whose size and diversity was unforeseen and probably unimaginable to Washington and his contemporaries, including those ordinary men who proved willing to risk their lives and fortunes so the United States could assume an independent place in the community of nations.

Notes

1. *Journals of the House of Representatives of Massachusetts*, LI, pt. 3 (1776) (Boston, 1984), 254; Stephen E. Patterson, *Political Parties in Revolu-*

tionary Massachusetts (Madison, Wis.: University of Wisconsin Press, 1973), 142.

2. Elbridge Gerry to James Warren, Philadelphia, March 26, 1776, in C. Harvey Gardiner, ed., *A Study in Dissent: The Warren-Gerry Correspondence, 1776–1792* (Carbondale, Ill.: Southern Illinois University Press, 1968), 12.

3. Worthington Chauncey Ford ed., *Journals of the Continental Congress,* V (1776) (Washington, 1906), 425.

4. In Peter Force, ed., *American Archives*, 4th ser., VI (Washington, 1846), 704 (Topsfield), 705 (Barnstable), and Francis Tiffany Bowles, *The Loyalty of Barnstable in the Revolution* (Cambridge, Mass.: 1924).

5. Force, ed., *American Archives*, VI, 706.

6. See, for example, Judith H. Shklar, *American Citizenship: The Quest for Inclusion* (Cambridge, Mass.: Harvard University Press, 1991).

7. Warren E. Leary, "Nation's Vital Documents Get Checkups," *New York Times*, 14 February 1995, Sec. C1 and C14.

8. North Carolina's early instructions to her congressional delegates empowering them to declare independence, April 12, 1776, and a set of instructions to their legislative representatives in favor of independence from the freeholders of James City County, Virginia, April 24, 1776, are in Force, ed., *American Archives,* 4th ser., V (Washington, 1844), 859, 1046–47. Many other documents referred to in the text are in *American Archives*, VI. See, for example, Virginia's instructions of May 15, 1776, 461–62; "A Declaration of the Delegates of Maryland," July 6, 1776, 1506–07; the Pennsylvania Conference of Committee's "Declaration on the subject of . . . Independence," June 24, 1776, 962–63; the resolution of Massachusetts towns 649, 698–706, and of Maryland county meetings, 1017–21; Presentment of the Grand Jury for the Cheraws District, S.C., May 20, 1776, 514–15, and the "humble Address of the General Committee of Mechanics in union, of the City and County of New York," May 29, 1776, 614–25. Virginia opened its new state constitution, adopted on June 29, 1776, with a formal declaration of independence, which Jefferson had drafted: See Julian P. Boyd, ed., *The Papers of Thomas Jefferson*, I (Princeton, N.J.: Princeton University Press, 1950), 377–79 and, for Jefferson's draft (which became his first draft of Congress's Declaration), 337–40 and 356–57.

9. Force ed., *American Archives*, 4th ser., VI, 704.

10. Force ed., *American Archives*, 4th ser., VI, 704.

11. Pennsylvania conference of committees, "Declaration on . . . Independence," June 24, 1776; Virginia convention instructions, May 15, 1776; Resolves of the town of Alford, Berkshire County, Mass., n.d., in Force ed., *American Archives*, 4th ser., VI, 962, 461, 629, 701; and also the instructions of James City County, Virginia, April 24, 1776, in *American Archives*, V, 1046–47. The James City instructions also suggest the colonists' two-mindedness on independence. They presented powerful arguments for separation and told the county's convention delegates to exert their "utmost abilities, toward dissolving the connection between America and Great Britain, totally, finally, and irrevocably." But in the midst of its radical rhetoric the document included a strange paren-

thetical qualification—"(provided no just and honourable terms are offered by the king)." *American Archives*, V, 1046–47.

12. On the events behind Jefferson's list of grievances, see Herbert Friedenwald, *The Declaration of Independence: An Interpretation and an Analysis* (New York: Da Capo Press, 1974; orig. pub. 1904).

13. See Lois Schwoerer, *The Declaration of Rights, 1689* (Baltimore, Md.: Johns Hopkins University Press, 1981).

14. Force, ed., *American Archives*, VI, 1018.

15. Pittsfield petition of December 16, 1775, in Robert J. Taylor, *Massachusetts, Colony to Commonwealth: Documents on the Formation of Its Constitution, 1775–1780* (Chapel Hill: University of North Carolina Press, 1961), 18; Jefferson's draft in Boyd, ed., *Jefferson Papers*, I, 357; and Pittsfield instructions in Force, ed., *American Archives*, VI, 649. (Emphasis added.)

16. Force, ed., *American Archives*, VI, 703; Pittsfield in Taylor, ed., *Massachusetts, Colony to Commonwealth*, 19.

17. This is not to deny that the event had important social and also economic effects, but that in the minds of contemporaries the challenge of founding a republican government was primary. The Revolution brought important reconceptualizations of American society, but its social implications were worked out over a longer period of time, and proposals for social change were often understood as ways better to fit the country to its republican government and to assure the republic's survival. See Pauline Maier, "The Transforming Impact of Independence, Reaffirmed: 1776 and the Definition of American Social Structure," in James A. Henretta et al, eds., *The Transformation of Early American History: Society, Authority, and Ideology* (New York: Knopf, 1991), 194–217.

18. Jefferson to Thomas Nelson, May 16, 1776, in Boyd, ed., *Jefferson Papers*, I, 292; Force, ed., *American Archives*, VI, 514–15.

19. Taylor, ed., *Massachusetts, Colony to Commonwealth*, 90–92, 112, 128 (quotation).

20. Rahe's book is perhaps the most prominent in an extensive literature reexamining the civic humanist or the classical republican interpretation of the Revolution. Of particular relevance here are Richard C. Sinopoli, *The Foundation of American Citizenship: Liberalism, the Constitution, and Civic Virtue* (New York: Oxford University Press, 1992) and Maier, "Transforming Impact of Independence," 205–13.

21. Quoted in John P. Roche, *The Early Development of United States Citizenship* (Ithaca, N.Y.: Cornell University Press, 1949), 23–24.

22. "Memorial of Rabbi Ger. Seixas," *Freeman's Journal* (Philadelphia, Pa.), (January 21, 1784).

23. The discussion of corporations here draws on Pauline Maier, "The Revolutionary Origins of the American Corporation," *William and Mary Quarterly*, 3d ser., L (1993), 51–84.

24. Maier, "Transforming Impact of Independence," 203–5, quotation at 203.

25. "An Act to Establish a College in the County of Berkshire . . . by the Name of Williams College," June 22, 1793, and "Petition to the General Court of Massachusetts from the Trustees of the Free School, May 22, 1792," in *Bicentennial Convocation of Williams College* from Arthur Latham Perry, *Williamstown and Williams College: A History* (Norwood, Mass.: Norwood Press, 1904), 214–7, 210–1. Those documents are also reprinted in the *Proceedings of the Massachusetts Historical Society*, CV, for 1993 (Boston, 1994), 154–59, and, more generally, the "Round Table" discussion by scholars and other documents on the founding of Williams, Proceedings of the Massachusetts Historical Society, pp. 124–164.

4

''Hearken Not to the Unnatural Voice'': Publius and the Artifice of Attachment

by Noah M. J. Pickus[1]

Most Americans do not find their deepest sense of attachment in the nation-state. The mediating institutions of our society—religious groups, ethnic associations, families—provide the affinity that a nation as large and variegated as the United States cannot hope to offer. We can be thankful that the United States does not try to substitute for those institutions. Most polities in which the strongest sense of community lies at the national level have eventually taught that citizens should ''think with their blood.''

Membership in the American polity is not, however, solely a matter of formal textual provisions governing eligibility and rights. United States citizenship also encompasses a notion of belonging to a political community. '' 'Belonging' is a soupy gerund,'' Kenneth Karst acknowledges. ''But the sense of belonging is no trivial matter. We all need it if we are to know ourselves and locate ourselves in the world.''[2]

The trouble is that the United States has never been able to assume that its citizens share any particular commitment to one another. Our polity, Michael Walzer notes, ''isn't undergirded by the cultural and religious commonalities that make for mutual trust.''[3] Americans therefore need to nurture a sense of belonging. The question, of course, is, Belonging based on what?

We cannot simply assert that a clear set of agreed-upon principles has formed the basis for our union. Belonging in the United States has often required more than merely assenting to a loose collection of political ideals. Our history is replete with conflicts *within* a set of ideas and not just been between one set of ideas and the institutions of the state.[4]

To say that this nation's commitment to a set of political principles has been both uneven and unclear is not to suggest that we cease offering accounts of why certain principles and virtues best comport with our constitutional project. But today there is a debate prior to the argument over what virtues are most appropriate to our constitutional order. Both scholarly and popular voices ask why we even need a shared sense of citizenship. While one wing of the multicultural movement seeks to expand the common civic tale that we tell ourselves, another wing denies the possibility or desirability of telling any common story. This denial finds fertile ground in a nation addicted to the nostrums of therapeutic individualism. Behind the disagreements over what story we ought to tell about America lies a dispute over whether we even need a common story.

In addition to discussing the virtues that contribute to a common citizenship, we must therefore also reaffirm the necessity of a shared sense of identity. Citizens have to regard belonging as itself important if talk of civic virtue is to find an attentive audience. I want to suggest that a reexamination of the Founders' arguments over citizenship and national identity offers a useful framework for understanding the perplexing issues involved in shaping citizens and forging attachment in a constitutional democracy. Rather than presenting an historical analysis, I emphasize what we can glean from Publius's view of citizenship by linking it to his more general theory of the constitutional order.[5]

I propose that Publius (and especially Madison) conceived citizenship to be neither a matter of cultural belonging nor of assenting to a settled set of political principles. For Publius, American citizenship meant attachment to a common identity that is itself subject to change. He tried to forge a shared identity without foreclosing deliberation over the nature of that identity. Publius's conception of citizenship provides compelling grounds for reestablishing a shared political identity as a central constitutional aspiration.

An Old Story: Self-Interest versus Virtue

Both supporters and detractors of Publius have tended to agree that he did not believe in shaping citizens. He is considered a stark realist who accepted "man as he is," naturally self-interested. On this view, the great invention of Publius's "new science of politics" was that it sought only to contain the damaging effects of our debased nature rather than to define or shape a particular kind of citizen. He designed a system that did not depend on the virtue of its citizenry. Indeed, by constructing a system that "let ambition counteract ambition," Publius denied the claim that a republic depended on the character and spirit of its people. Instead, he adopted Montesquieu's reliance on institutions operating in a large commercial republic that encompassed a wide range of interests.

This plan displaced both the classical and the Christian view of character formation that stressed "frugality, industry, temperance and simplicity."[6] "The aim of political organization was not to educate men," Sheldon Wolin comments in summarizing this view of Madison, "but to deploy them; not to alter their moral character but to arrange institutions in such a manner that human drives would cancel each other."[7] Wolin's position is shared by other liberal and radical political theorists, as well as by such historians as Charles Beard, Vernon Parrington, Gordon Wood, Richard Hofstadter, and John Patrick Diggins. Conservative thinkers like George Will provide a similar diagnosis, treating Madison's vision of American identity as the progenitor of an interest group liberalism that obscures the importance of virtue. This vision "secur[es] its citizens," Hadley Arkes writes, "mainly in their liberty to pursue their own, private interests."[8] From this perspective, commerce is the only bond of union.

Some scholars have tried to counter this view of Madison by pointing to his obvious belief in a conception of the public good (factions are "adverse to the rights of other citizens, or to the permanent and aggregate interests of the community") and in the importance of virtue in attaining that good ("the vigilant and manly spirit which actuates the people of America"). Some locate a more positive conception of citizenship in Publius's references to his "esteem and confidence" in citizens and to the "ability and virtue" needed from occupants of political office. "Is there no virtue among us?" asked Madison. "If there be not we are in a wretched situation. No theoretical checks—no form of government can render us secure. To suppose that any form of government will secure liberty or happiness without any virtue in the people, is a chimerical idea."[9] And, more famously, from *Federalist 55*:

As there is a degree of depravity in mankind which requires a certain degree of circumspection and distrust, so there are other qualities in human nature which justify a certain portion of esteem and confidence. Republican government presupposes the existence of these qualities in a higher

degree than any other form. Were the pictures which have been drawn by
the political jealousy of some among us faithful likenesses of the human
character, the inference would be that there is not sufficient virtue among
men for self-government.[10]

From this perspective, the only sense of national identity was one com-
mensurate with the degree of virtue already possessed by the people.

Madison's own arguments support versions of his system that stress
the importance of commerce and those that focus on character. Much
of his defense of the new Constitution stressed the role of self-interest.
Yet, at critical moments, the proposed system appeared predicated on
the presence of a virtuous citizenry. This apparent disjunction can be
resolved partly by noting the difference between the system Madison
advocated in *The Federalist* and the views he held in general. Finding
no orderly examination of citizenship in *The Federalist*, scholars have
scrutinized a variety of other statements by the Founders. They have
argued that, contrary to the portrait of Madison as a cold-blooded cele-
brator of atomistic individualism, he devoted much of his life to encouraging virtuous habits and community life. As James Q. Wilson recently
explained, Madison's "conclusion was that man is sufficiently virtuous
and deliberative as to make it possible to design and operate a constitution that supplies and maintains that system of restraints."[11]

What all these attempts to reconcile Madison's divergent views have
in common is a conviction that his system plays little or no role in
shaping a new citizenry and a distinctly American identity. Whether
scholars believe that Madison depended primarily on the clash of ambition or assumed the natural presence of virtue, they agree that changing
human nature does *not* constitute the purpose of his constitutional design. I think their agreement has obscured Publius's efforts to shape
fundamentally the kind of citizens he thought a constitutional democracy required.

The dichotomy between Madisonian self-interest and Madisonian virtue functions on the same side of a broader question: whether a constitutional democracy requires a certain kind of citizen. The self-interest/
virtue debate also falls on the same side of a subsidiary question: To
what extent ought political and cultural institutions play a role in forming such a citizen? Publius and many other of the Founders in fact
considered the task of molding citizens critical to the success of their
new enterprise. "The people," Madison wrote in 1792, "ought to be
enlightened, to be awakened, to be united. . . ."[12] Political, legal, and
educational institutions, as well as language and literature, were considered instruments essential to the formation of constitutional democrats.

Despite relying on self-interest, Publius's mechanisms of republican government were also meant to elicit a degree of moral growth through political experience. Steven Macedo delineates the main elements in this conception of political virtue: the "broadening of self-interest through rational foresight and cooperativeness; a love of freedom, jealousy of rights, and pride in being self-supporting citizens," instilled by liberal political culture; and, owing to democratic representation, "relatively well-informed and enlightened characters who make the law."[13] Ralph Lerner identifies specific personal traits that the early Federalist justices sought to inculcate. A citizen should learn to be "plainspoken, self-possessed, manly in a quiet rather than gallus-tugging fashion; jealous of his rights, but aware of his duties and the self-esteem of others."[14] Through their charges to the jury and later through their reasoned opinions, the justices sought to "introduce the language of the law into the vulgar tongue . . . [and] transfer to the minds of citizens the modes of thought lying behind legal language and the notions of right fundamental to the regime."[15]

Thomas Pangle reminds us that many Founders were "troubled by the depressing awareness that the cultivation of commercialism and individualism was at odds with the requirements of public spirit and patriotic devotion."[16] Following the ratification debates, they began to focus on moral (and religious) education as a means of promoting civic virtue. Presidents Washington, Jefferson, Madison, and John Quincy Adams sent messages to Congress calling for a national university that would, as Washington explained, assimilate "the principles, opinions, and manners of our Country men. . . ."[17] William F. Harris II, describes how "members of the American founding generation [designed] universities . . . to fit the mental habits of the Constitution's citizens to the new forms of political life. The University of Virginia (1819) and the University of Michigan (1817), as prime examples, were both overtly so conceived."[18] Benjamin Rush imagined an entire educational system, not just the universities, that would "render the mass of people more homogeneous, and thereby fit them more easily for uniform and peaceable government."[19]

Further evidence abounds that Publius and many other Founders considered it a central task to create a citizen whose fundamental values and patterns of thought coincided with the principles undergirding free government. Benjamin Franklin, for instance, sought in his *Autobiography* to teach by example the importance of establishing a "Method" for regulating future conduct in life. Lerner demonstrates how Franklin wanted the individual gradually to " 'acquire the Habitude' of all the virtues'' and to prepare " 'the Minds of the People' for new proposals.''[20] Noah Webster offered his American dictionary "as a corollary to his theories of the new American republic, giving the Constitution's citizens an established domain of speech with a limited range of spellings and meanings.''[21] James Q. Wilson is right that Madison thought humans both self-interested and virtuous. But this balanced judgment should not blind us to the many ways in which the system Madison designed sought to produce a certain kind of citizen.

Attachment to a Common Identity

I want to focus on one idea Publius sought to inculcate in a new citizenry. This idea lies at the heart of his conception of citizenship and American identity. In his defense of the proposed constitution, Publius attempted to foster attachment to a common identity among the ratifiers by creating a belief that the colonists actually constituted one people. The vehemence of the Anti-Federalists' objections suggests that this effort was not just strategic rhetoric. Publius's bid to establish a sense of peoplehood was intimately linked with his view of the allegiance required by a constitutional democracy. His claims were rooted in his understanding of the role constitutions played in engendering attachment to the polity. By examining the Federalists' and the Anti-Federalists' divergent conceptions of law and the role of constitutions, we can see how deeply Publius sought to create a new identity that would affect the colonists way of thinking. He tried to generate a collective identity that would undergird a common citizenship.

In recent years, scholars have tended to mute the differences between the Federalists and the Anti-Federalists. While acknowledging a variety of distinctions between (and within) the two groups, they have been inclined to agree, correctly, I think, that both groups "believed themselves heirs of an authentic republican tradition.''[22] Each sought to preserve rights and extend liberties, albeit in different ways. On this view, the Federalists possessed some concern for a virtuous citizenry and the Anti-Federalists were cognizant of the serious weaknesses inherent in the Articles of Confederation. This consensual account is an important corrective to earlier views that dismissed the Anti-Federalists' contribution to the Constitution and ignored their role as representatives of an important alternative in American political thought. But too much emphasis on what the two groups shared in common misses their deep divisions over Publius's attempt to create a sense of peoplehood.

For many of the Anti-Federalists, law is found rather than created. It memorializes settled practices and codifies existing rules; it does not consciously make new rules. Indeed, Centinel proclaims that "it is the genius of the common law to resist innovation."[23]

Many of the Anti-Federalists thus treated the Constitution as a symbol of memory, an historical artifact. Because law is an accumulation of pieces rather than a systematically designed whole, they objected to the Federalists' presentation of the proposed Constitution as a unified system that had to be adopted comprehensively. Instead, they treated the proposed Constitution as a series of discrete recommendations designed to bring about incremental changes.[24]

This understanding of law and the role of constitutions fits well with the Anti-Federalists' conception of civic education and the formation of citizens. "The Anti-Federalist," explained Herbert Storing, "thought of the whole organization of the polity as having an educative function. The small republic was seen as a school of citizenship as much as a scheme of government. An important part . . . of their argument for a federal bill of rights was the educative function of such a document in reminding the citizen of the ends of civil government and in strengthening his attachment to it."[25] For the Anti-Federalists, civic education meant training in truths already acknowledged. They envisioned the constitution and the structure of the polity as molding citizens to preexisting norms and beliefs.

Agrippa explained the basis for this approach by offering a theory of the genesis of politics in which governments are not made but exist naturally. "Wherever we find a settlement of men, we find also some appearance of government. That state of government is therefore as natural to mankind as a state of society."[26] The earliest form of government was practiced, he imagined, by American Indians in which "the whole authority of government is vested in the whole tribe" and influence stems from reputations for valor and wisdom. The next stage of the historical development of mankind finds authority transferred to kings who are limited in their power only by rules of succession. Moses then established a government of more limited powers, which stood for five centuries until the people demanded a king so as to be like other nations. But "instead of changing the administration, they madly changed their constitution." As a result, "however [the Israelites] might flatter themselves with the idea, that a high-spirited people could get back the power again when they pleased; they never did get it back."[27]

From this "general view of the state of mankind," Agrippa derived the principle that, once a people delegates power to a government, they cannot reclaim any unlisted rights. If a people commit themselves to a comprehensive plan, they cannot turn back: "All the powers of government originally reside in the body of the people; and that when they appoint certain persons to administer the government, they delegate all the powers of government not expressly reserved."[28] Writing a constitution with a pen dipped in the ink of an Anti-Federalist science of politics means writing down the rights already possessed by a people. In their view, a constitutional text should reflect rather than shape a people's culture. It should not govern relations between people or regulate the people's control of government. "[A] constitution," says Agrippa, "does not in itself imply any more than a declaration of the relation which the different parts of government bear to each other, but does not in any degree imply security to the rights of individuals."[29] Constitutions, in short, constitute very little.

Publius's solution to the dilemma of how to regulate conflicting interests without destroying liberty is well known. He argued that allowing a multitude of interests to clash over an extended republic would limit the authority of any one interest. It is less recognized that Publius also thought such conflict posed special dangers in a society held together by few natural bonds. To moderate the effects of difference and diversity, he believed a polity should inculcate attachment to a new constitutional identity. The Anti-Federalists' conception of citizenship, he worried, could not fulfill this task. The Anti-Federalists would only seek to educate citizens on the basis of settled doctrine and practices. Their conception of citizenship could not create common beliefs and practices among culturally dissimilar and self-interested individuals. As a result, Publius feared the colonists could only regard one another as strangers unwilling to shoulder collective burdens.

For Publius, however, a legally ordered polity was not dependent on the cultural homogeneity of its people. Instead, he contended it was possible to create a republic through "reflection and choice." This phrase has lost some of its impact through repetition. For Publius it meant that the entire Federalist enterprise depended on an act of informed imagination, a projection onto the future of what their two-dimensional textual construction might look like when raised to the three-dimensionality of a polity. All constitutions must, of course, be translated into institutional practice. But Publius meant the process of translation to engender a manner of thinking at a new level of meaning and consciousness. More than merely following the dictates of the written text, individuals would have to learn to think holistically, to imagine a complete system rather than separable parts.

For Publius, the first step in the process entailed creating a world in which individuals recognized each other as participants in a common project, as fellow citizens. Hence, the most fundamental belief that Publius sought to instantiate was that the colonists constituted one people. New citizens would have to regard the Constitution's authority as rooted in their collective status as a people.

To be sure, Jay at one point links successful nation-building to the presence of a homogeneous culture:

> Providence has been pleased to give this one connected country to one united people—a people descended from the same ancestors, speaking the same language, professing the same religion, attached to the same principles of government, very similar in manners and customs.[30]

Jay's claim was strained, and he must have known it to be overstated. The extent of national consciousness was itself at issue during the ratification debates. Beyond obvious sectional differences, Jay's pronouncement glossed over significant differences among Germans in Pennsylvania, Catholics in Maryland, Quakers in Pennsylvania and New Jersey, and Scotch-Irish Presbyterians scattered throughout several states, not to mention blacks and Native Americans. Benjamin Franklin undercut any pretensions to homogeneity when he asked: "Why should Pennsylvania, founded by the English, become a colony of aliens who will shortly be so numerous as to Germanize us instead of Anglifying them, and will never adopt our Language or Customs any more than they can acquire our complexion?" And Madison himself admitted that, while

> [i]t was true as had been observed we had not among us those hereditary distinctions of rank which were a great source of the contests in the ancient governments as well as the modern States of Europe, nor those extremes of wealth or poverty which characterize the latter . . . , we cannot however be regarded even at this time, as one homogeneous mass, in which every thing that affects a part will affect in the same manner the whole.[31]

The logic of Publius's constitutional theory suggests a different view than the Anti-Federalist conception of citizenship that Jay's claim seems to represent. Publius's grand strategy to transform colonists into citizens required them to become committed to a common identity. He struggled to clearly define the content of that identity. His writings do not discuss ethnic diversity and conflict in nation-building. But Publius did not ignore the dilemmas presented by the colonists' heterogeneity.

The entire argument of *The Federalist* itself constituted an attempt to overcome the colonists' deeply rooted habit of thinking in regional, ethnic, and religious parts by elaborating a history of "the people." We begin to see Publius's artifice as a constitution maker, his artfulness and his skill, when he utilizes a great jumble of principles, culture, and experience to portray subnational identities as less real than what the colonists share. "Hearken not to the unnatural voice," he warns,

> which tells you that the people of America, knit together as they are by so many cords of affection, can no longer live together as members of the same family; can no longer continue the mutual guardians of their mutual happiness; can no longer be fellow-citizens of one great, respectable, and flourishing empire. The kindred blood which flows in the veins of American citizens, the mingled blood which they have shed in defense of their sacred rights, consecrate their Union and excite horror at the idea of their becoming aliens, rivals, enemies. And if novelties are to be shunned, believe me, the most alarming of all novelties, the most wild of all projects, the most rash of all attempts, is that of rending us in pieces in order to preserve our liberties and promote our happiness.[32]

Publius asserts that the colonists share a distinctive bond of affection, responsibility, and blood. Further, they possess a unique nature, a "genius," as a people: "It is evident that no other form [than republican] would be reconcilable with the genius of the people of America; with the fundamental principles of the Revolution; or with that honorable determination which animates every votary of freedom to rest all our political experiments on the capacity of mankind for self-government."[33] What they believe ("the capacity of mankind for self-government"), as well as who they were and what crucible they have passed through (the "kindred blood" that has become "mingled blood") suggest who they have already become. *The Federalist* looks outward into recent history and inward into the Revolution's principles to invoke a people who possess a specific genius.

Publius's strategy, then, lays the groundwork for asking this newly constructed people to envision itself possessing a certain institutional form. In the closing paragraph of the final *Federalist* paper, Hamilton proclaims: "A NATION, without a NATIONAL GOVERNMENT, is in my view, an awful spectacle."[34] Madison explains the basis for this "awful spectacle" by arguing that a people does not truly possess a political identity until it has achieved an institutional form that provides a public manifestation of its peoplehood. The spirit, or genius, of the people that Madison has invoked now needs a body. The text and the institutions it envisions will make you, he says, a real constitutional people, which is what you wanted to be.

The Anti-Federalists' sense of time is linear. Free and independent persons formed a society and became a people who then established a government by means of a written constitution.[35] Publius's sense of time is more like a möbius strip. Despite the colonists' manifest differences, he justified the specific institutional form he proposed by reference to the kind of people "Americans" were already. But as we have just seen, some ratifiers' conception of who those Americans were is precisely what the constitutional text and *The Federalist* had sought to establish. The people and the constitutional text exist in a reciprocal relation in which one cannot survive without the other. The Constitution cannot be justified on textual grounds because it does not yet exist and so possesses no independent authority as a constitution. Publius's account of the people's standing and stature is meant to provide that authority. The people, in turn, are meant to accept the text's constraints because they authorized the project themselves. But, ultimately, they know that they have authorized the project only because the text and the account given of it by Publius tells them so. The Constitution bends back on itself, referring the text to its origins in the people and the origins of the people to the text. In this manner, Publius sought to generate a collective identity as a basis for a common citizenship.[36]

There is a degree of inventiveness, or, to put it bluntly, of subterfuge, in Publius's efforts. "We the people" do not exist naturally. The "We" must be nursed into being. In doing so, Publius has not provided an especially clear statement of what constitutes that people's identity as Americans. He mixes principles, culture, experience, and fellow-feeling in a manner that makes it difficult to discern any sharp definition. But that artifice is precisely what Publius deemed necessary. In an extended republic encompassing a diversity of identities and interests, citizenship must be understood in terms of attachment to a common identity. It must be valued long before it can be more fully understood.

Determining What Is Held in Common

Publius did not, however, see American citizenship simply as dependent on the invention of an unchanging conception of national identity. Creating a sense of peoplehood was only the first step in the process of causing individuals to think holistically, to imagine a complete system rather than separable parts. We can see the second and equally important step when we recognize that, for Publius, a sense of peoplehood is not meant to foreclose deliberation over the nature of that people's common identity. Indeed, ongoing deliberation over who a people are and ought to be is central to determining what that people actually share in common. This key point is illustrated by Publius's opposition to a Bill of Rights. He feared that a list of rights appended to the constitutional text would teach citizens that no deliberation was necessary as to the proper relation between power and rights in different eras and situations. As a result, the "reflection and choice" necessary to define what is held in common would atrophy.

The Anti-Federalists believed that a Bill of Rights would play an important educative role. They argued that such a bill, preferably placed in the preamble of the Constitution, would reassure those uncertain about the proposed government, help in specifying limits on that government, and, most important, remind the new citizens of their system's fundamental precepts by recognizing those principles, as the Federal Farmer put it, "in the front page of every family book."[37] Their science of politics posited that rights exist in an ocean of powers. To protect rights they must therefore be enumerated. Scholars such as Herbert Storing and Edmund Morgan, who follow the Anti-Federalists in holding that a constitution is a contract between a people and its government, have turned a skeptical eye on the Federalists' disinclination to specify the terms of the contract. They find the Federalists' arguments "a bit sophistical."[38]

Publius's objection to the Bill of Rights is more compelling than sophistical. It derives partly from a belief in limited government. "In Europe, charters of liberty have been granted by power," Madison explained. "America has set the example and France has followed it, of charters of power granted by liberty."[39] A Bill of Rights is therefore unnecessary: "For why declare that things shall not be done which there is no power to do?"[40] The Constitution itself provides for an ethos of limited government and is, "in every rational sense, and to every useful purpose, A BILL OF RIGHTS."[41] Such a bill introduced into or appended onto the text would merely provide a concrete statement of the larger principle. Moreover, beyond being redundant, specifying rights could imply that these rights were exceptions to a general grant of governmental powers, whereas in fact the government was one of specific enumerated powers. A Bill of Rights might thus cause damage by appearing to limit individual rights to those listed.[42]

Publius's objection to the Bill of Rights was, however, based on an even deeper concern than that rights would be limited. He feared the capacity to define what is held in common would diminish if an Anti-Federalist science of politics found its way into the constitutional text. This fear was based on his conception that power and rights do not always exist in a zero-sum relation. For Publius, increasing power does not necessarily diminish rights. Instead, by creating a whole greater than the sum of its parts, a polity can generate surplus power that protects rights.[43] Collectivizing political energy can, in fact, help to overcome some of the difficulties arising from faction and insurrection. "The vigor of government is essential to the security of liberty," Hamilton proclaims, and, quoting Montesquieu, argues that the proposed constitution envisages " 'a kind of assemblage of societies that constitute a new one, capable of increasing, by means of new association, till they arrive to such a degree of power as to be able to provide for security of the united body.' "[44]

In *Federalist* 9, Hamilton specifies the various advances in the science of politics that make for this capacity to generate surplus power and explains why this increase in power protects rather than tyrannizes rights. He particularly singles out the "ENLARGEMENT of the ORBIT." Those who depend on Montesquieu's argument for the "necessity of a contracted territory for a republican government" fail to recognize that Montesquieu was referring to societies far smaller than even the present colonial states. Instead, by "extending the republic" Montesquieu explained how a new union would prevent the usurpation of rights: if a single member attempted to usurp power he could not attain equal authority in all states; if he grasps power in one state, the others will become alarmed; if a popular insurrection occurs in one state the others can quell it; and more modest abuses in a single state can be cured by the soundness in others.

This understanding that the relation between power and rights is not necessarily zero-sum enables us to see the pivotal *Federalist* 10 as the context for Publius's opposition to a Bill of Rights. Treated on its own, this essay is most often read from the "bottom up," from an analysis of human nature as essentially self-interested to Madison's plan to control the effect of factions by letting them clash in an extended republic. This argument usually serves as the linchpin to the charge against Madison that he takes human nature as given and does not try to change it. And, indeed, Madison did believe that self-interest drives faction and that the extended republic helps to sap the effect of faction.

But placed in the context of *The Federalist*'s larger strategy, and especially in proximity to Hamilton's argument in *Federalist* 9, we might also read number 10 from the "top down," from the "wholeness" argument that power and rights do not exist in a zero-sum relation. Hamilton's discussion of the extended republic's capacity to control the effect of faction operates as a subset of this "wholeness" argument. Madison's consideration of the extended republic is, therefore, notable not simply for its account of the sources of faction but because it builds on Hamilton's explication of the purpose of "enlarging the orbit." *Federalist* 10 is designed to get potential ratifiers to envisage such a system by establishing the principle of the whole over the parts and explaining how, by following this principle, the method of enlarging the orbit collectivizes energy in such a way as to moderate the effects of faction.

This reading of *Federalist* 10 enables us to understand better Publius's opposition to the Bill of Rights and how that opposition reveals his belief that what a people hold in common must be subject to change. The process of imagining sufficient energy to protect rights described in number 10 is meant to shift the colonists away from thinking in terms of parts and as members of subgroups. It attempts to make the polity self-regulating by depending for political wisdom on citizens' reflection on the polity's nature and historical development, rather than on specific textual provisions. If power and rights do not exist in a zero-sum relation, then argument is required to demonstrate what balance ought to be struck in a particular situation. Questions about the nature or extent of a right or the limits or reach of governmental power must be settled by deliberation among a people. What, for instance, Hamilton asks, is liberty of the press?

> Who can give it any definition which would not leave the utmost latitude for evasion? I hold it to be impracticable; and from this I infer that its security, whatever fine declarations may be inserted in any constitution respecting it, must altogether depend on public opinion, and on the general spirit of the people and of government. And here, after all, must we seek for the only solid basis of all our rights.[45]

Similarly, Madison maintains that,

> If it be asked, what is to restrain the House of Representatives from making legal discrimination in favor of themselves and a particular class of the society? I answer: the genius of the whole system; the nature of just and constitutional laws; and, above all, the vigilant and manly spirit which actuates the people of America—a spirit which nourishes freedom, and in return is nourished by it.[46]

Publius repudiated the Anti-Federalists' view that only enumerated rights can be secure. He thought their dependence on specific textual provisions incorrectly assumed a people always knew the meaning of their rights. He therefore feared the Anti-Federalists' position would curtail deliberation over the relation between rights and powers. Indeed, he worried that their focus on a fixed national creed would diminish citizens' capacity to deliberate based on "reflection and choice."[47] As a result, Publius doubted citizens would be able to clarify their commonalities when they confronted new dilemmas or revisited lingering controversies.

Publius objected to a single, unchanging conception of belonging in America. He suspected a conformity of opinion would retard rather than enhance allegiance to a common identity. To make solid commitments to the principles undergirding the polity, citizens had to understand, and repudiate, alternatives to those principles. If citizens lacked real choices, they would also lack commitment to the polity. Because little would appear at stake in vigorously supporting the polity, citizens would never have to strongly devote themselves to it. Tocqueville worried over this same dilemma when he warned that, beneath the superficial diversity apparent among citizens of a liberal democracy, the pressure to conform, to remain a part of "the people," threatened to subvert their attachment to the principles undergirding the polity:

> I know of no country in which there is so little independence of mind and real freedom of discussion as in America. . . . The majority lives in the perpetual utterance of self-applause, and there are certain truths which the Americans can learn only from strangers or from experience.[48]

Some societies that have established the state as the preeminent site of allegiance, such as those under fascist rule, have been able to sustain a high level of loyalty. Remaining a good citizen of other communities, such as religious ones, may depend far more on reverence than reason. The thrust of Publius's argument about the nature and importance of "reflection and choice" is that preserving space for alternatives to the present order is necessary in a constitutional democracy committed to human liberty. Reasoned exploration of the principles a citizen reveres can shake that person's faith. But that risk is necessary if citizens are to avoid the dangers of complacency and flaccidity.

The search for a common identity depends upon deliberation. Publius's conception of thinking holistically does not forestall conflicting interpretations or compel individuals to think alike. After all, deliberation depends upon diversity because to reflect and then choose requires that one consider alternative possibilities. This means that what a people have in common may change. Thinking holistically *does*, however, require an attempt to convince others that one's interpretation is not simply an announcement of preference or a selfish act designed to circumvent a shared political identity.

Bradley Carter and Joseph Kobylka point out, for instance, that Madison, in opposing the Alien and Sedition Acts, sought to secure all the people's approval for his position. "The test of the acts was not the immediate political will in *one* state, but rather the compatibility of the Acts, *in the public mind*, with the principles underlying the political community of all states."[49] Three decades later, Madison compared his approach to South Carolina's assertion that it had authority to nullify federal laws, and withdraw from the polity, without attempting to persuade the rest of the union. He condemned South Carolina for simply announcing its position rather than commending it to the union as a whole.[50] Stephen Elkin captures Madison's position when he writes:

> It is not necessary that citizens be either similarly situated, as the civic republican idea implies, or motivated in so strict a fashion. . . . Citizens only have to be disposed to believe that there is something more to public choice than combining private interests and that those who participate in the making of those choices (who may be themselves) must be held to a standard of advocacy that requires that they talk in larger terms.[51]

In Publius's view, the constant search for defining a people's "permanent and aggregate interests" influences the health of a constitutional democracy. The ideal citizen should not retreat into an Anti-Federalist defense of small, homogeneous communities or into a thin, minimalist position that champions tolerance as the preeminent good. Doing so undermines the constant effort to bind citizens together that being a free people requires. "Belief that it is possible for the Constitution to guide constitutional decisions does not require actual agreement about the meaning of constitutional language," observes Sotirios Barber. "[I]t requires only a belief in the possibility of agreement. . . . [T]hose who believe it can mean nothing in particular cannot take it seriously as law."[52]

The process of finding agreement beneath differences sustains attachment to a common citizenship. This process challenges the resignation of those who feel themselves outside the dominant identity. It offers them the opportunity to alter the core of that identity. This search for agreement also challenges the complacency of those comfortably inside the dominant identity. It compels them to acknowledge the presence of alternatives to the present order. For both groups, the emphasis on find-ing agreement beneath differences, on the relative fluidity of a common identity, means that something valuable is at stake in the present system.

This model of citizenship does not deny that certain rights and values may be fundamental to the polity. Quite the opposite—it assumes that the conversation is about substantive commitments. American national identity is more than a matter of process, of infinite ''conversations'' in which nothing gets decided. The Declaration of Independence treated equality and the right to life, liberty, and the pursuit of happiness as self-evident truths, not as suggestions. The new nation's conception of citizenship as defined by consent rather than dissent promoted a radi-cally innovative doctrine of membership. The Founders clearly intended that the Constitution and the citizenry it formed would usher in a new era of individual freedom and popular sovereignty.

This model of citizenship simply acknowledges that those commit-ments can be changed. In signing the Emancipation Proclamation, Abraham Lincoln redefined the meaning of property.[53] Citizenship therefore represents a commitment to make, and to be bound by, argu-ments about the nature of our common identity. In this view, the consti-tutional text serves as a proxy for moral certainty. It does not displace that which it claims to stand for, the sovereign people and their affirma-tions of inalienable rights. Rather, it represents what that people recog-nize as the basis for their polity. Any values attributed to the constitu-tional text are therefore subject to change. This fluidity does not mean that the text is so indeterminate that it is impossible to talk about the ''we.'' Instead, it suggests that even in the face of pluralism and uncer-tainty, shared meaning is possible. Those who doubt the possibility of a truly common national identity undermine the purpose of a polity ordered by a written constitution. They accept our disagreements as if those differences reflect a natural, inviolate state of affairs. From Publi-us's perspective, the fact of difference is one reason *to* form a political community that binds people without making them idol worshippers.

Madison's admonition in *Federalist* 37 that language is a ''cloudy medium'' sought to spur exploration and explanation, not to justify call-ing off the search for meaning.[54] Madison was impressed with what the authors of the constitutional text accomplished *despite* the difficulties of forging political agreement. ''The real wonder is that so many diffi-culties should have been surmounted,'' he reflects, ''and surmounted with a unanimity almost as unprecedented as it must have been unex-pected.''[55] A constitutional text fixes meanings, even if only temporar-

ily and subject to alteration. In doing so, it creates institutions that can
be used. It also creates individuals who can recognize one another as
fellow citizens based on their status as cointerpreters.

Reestablishing the Search

Publius did not entirely succeed in fostering a common national identity. He certainly could not resolve the division between state and national loyalties. Nor did Publius's design indicate whether political participation would ever extend beyond propertied white males. He also
failed to clarify how much cultural homogeneity would be necessary to
sustain the polity. Despite his approval of relatively open immigration
policies, Publius sometimes relied on an imagined cultural unity. But
the logic of Publius's vision of citizenship in a constitutional order reveals a more complex view than that suggested by his unstable mixture
of principles and culture.

Although Publius counted on and hoped for a degree of genuine patriotism, his model did not demand constant self-sacrifice or an end to
pursuing personal interest. Publius's constitutional design did not primarily seek to improve human nature in the sense of making individuals
more virtuous in Classical, Christian, or Rousseauist terms. But his design did intend to change people, to shape them by making them part
of something larger. The transformation Publius sought would create a
polity bound together by more than a modicum of sameness, virtue, or
commerce. By beginning to think of themselves as a people, the citizens
of the new republic would seek in public to commend different positions to their fellow citizens on the basis of the logic and principles of
free government. Publius sought to give the colonists a common identity as citizens, an identity rooted both in the "fact" of their peoplehood
and in the necessity of deliberating over the nature of that people, over
what rights and powers were consonant with continuing to be a free
people.

What should constitute the main virtues in a shared understanding of
citizenship is a complex question. How to determine those virtues without imposing too narrow a vision on an increasingly heterogeneous people presents an even more delicate problem. But the argument over
which virtues best fit our nature as a people requires agreement that it
still makes sense to talk about being one people. Advocates of influen-
tial ideas in both the scholarly and popular worlds challenge that agreement. In questioning the idea that it is both possible and desirable to

search for a common identity these voices do not just reject some specific conception of citizenship. They reject the entire search for a common conception. We should follow Publius's lead and reestablish the ground for that search.

Notes

1. I am grateful to Walter F. Murphy, Jennifer L. Hochschild, William F. Harris II, Murray Dry, Wayne D. Moore, Linda S. Bosniak, Robert C. Lieberman, Trudi J. Abel, and the editors of this volume for helpful comments. I also benefitted from presenting earlier versions of this article at the 1992 American Political Science Association meeting and at a colloquium at Princeton University sponsored by the Bouton Lecture Fund.

2. Kenneth L. Karst, *Belonging to America: Equal Citizenship and the Constitution* (New Haven: Yale University Press, 1989), ix.

3. Michael Walzer, "What Does It Mean to Be an 'American'?", *Social Research* 57, no. 3 (Fall 1990): 602.

4. See Rogers M. Smith, "Beyond Tocqueville, Myrdal, and Hartz: The Multiple Traditions in America," *American Political Science Review.* 87, no. 3 (September 1993).

5. To invoke the name Publius too casually is to elide a series of disagreements over the coherence of a fictitious persona. I do not want to rehearse the "split personality" debate here. Clearly, Madison, Hamilton, and Jay differed in a number of ways and each altered some of his views over time. Still, by concentrating on Publius as a single voice I hope to show that, whatever the disagreements among his creators, a coherent (if unfinished) approach to the formation of citizens emerges.

6. Gordon Wood, *The Creation of the American Republic, 1776–1787* (Chapel Hill, N.C.: University of North Carolina Press, 1969), 52.

7. Sheldon Wolin, *Politics and Vision: Continuity and Innovation in Western Political Thought* (Boston: Little, Brown, 1960), 389.

8. Hadley, Arkes, *Beyond the Constitution* (Princeton, N.J.: Princeton University Press, 1990), 65.

9. James Madison, Virginia Convention, June 20, 1788, in Saul K. Padaver, ed., *The Complete Madison: His Basic Writings* (New York: Harper, 1953), 48.

10. James Madison, *The Federalist Papers* 55, ed. Clinton Rossiter (New York: New American Library, 1961), 346.

11. James Q. Wilson, "Interests and Deliberation in the American Republic, or, Why James Madison Would Never Have Received the James Madison Award," *PS: Political Science and Politics* 23, no. 4 (December 1990), 558–62.

12. James Madison, "Who are the Best Keepers of the People's Liberties?", *National Gazette*, December 20, 1792, in Gaillard Hunt, ed. *The Writings of*

James Madison (New York: G. P. Putnam and Sons, 1902–1910), vol. 6, 120, 121.

13. Steven Macedo, *Liberal Virtues: Citizenship, Virtue and Community in Liberal Constitutionalism* (New York: Oxford University Press, 1990), 140.

14. Ralph Lerner, *The Thinking Revolutionary: Principle and Practice in the New Republic* (Ithaca, N.Y.: Cornell University Press, 1979), 102.

15. Lerner, *The Thinking Revolutionary*, 136.

16. Thomas Pangle, "Commentary," in Robert A. Goldwin, Art Kaufman, William A. Schambra, eds., *Forging Unity Out of Diversity: The Approaches of Eight Nations* (Washington, D.C.: American Enterprise Institute, 1989), 98. See also Pangle, *The Ennobling of Democracy: The Postmodern Age* (Baltimore, Md.: Johns Hopkins University Press, 1992), chapter 9.

17. Quoted in Pangle, "Commentary," 87–88.

18. William F. Harris II, *The Interpretable Constitution* (Baltimore, Md.: Johns Hopkins University Press, 1993), 59 n. 19.

19. Quoted in Pangle, "Commentary," 88.

20. Lerner, *The Thinking Revolutionary*, 49–50.

21. Harris, *The Interpretable Constitution*, 102 n. 14.

22. Linda K. Kerber, "The Revolutionary Generation: Ideology, Politics, and Culture in the Early Republic," 42, in Eric Foner, ed., *The New American History* (Philadelphia: Temple University Press, 1990). See also James W. Ceaser, *Liberal Democracy and Political Science* (Baltimore, Md.: Johns Hopkins University Press, 1990), chapter 1.

23. The letters of Centinel, October 5, 1787, in Cecelia Kenyon, ed., *The Anti-Federalists* (Boston: Northeastern University Press, 1966), 4.

24. See, especially, the letters of Centinel.

25. Herbert Storing, *What the Anti-Federalists Were For* (Chicago: University of Chicago Press, 1981), 21.

26. Agrippa, in Kenyon, *The Anti-Federalists*, 148.

27. Agrippa, in Kenyon, *The Anti-Federalists*, 149.

28. Agrippa, in Kenyon, *The Anti-Federalists*, 149.

29. Agrippa, in Kenyon, *The Anti-Federalists*, 149.

30. Jay, *The Federalist Papers* 2, ed. Clinton Rossiter (1961), 38.

31. Max Farrand, ed., *Records of the Federal Convention of 1787* (New Haven, Conn.: Yale University Press, 1911), vol. I, 422.

32. Madison, *The Federalist Papers* 14, 103–4.

33. Madison, *The Federalist Papers* 39, 242.

34. Alexander Hamilton, *The Federalist Papers* 85, 527.

35. Walter Berns mistakenly attributes this position to Madison when he posits that "before there can be a legitimate government there must be a people to institute it, and before there can be a people there must be a compact among persons. . . ." For Berns's Madison, the Constitution operates as little more than an instrument of a people already formed by the noble words of the Declaration. What Berns misses, I think, is the extent to which the Constitution itself

played a role in creating that people. See *Taking the Constitution Seriously* (New York: Simon and Schuster, 1987), 23.

36. For further discussion of the relationship between text and peoplehood, see Harris, *The Interpretable Constitution*, 48, 73–83.

37. Federal Farmer, January 20, 1788, in Herbert J. Storing, *The Anti-Federalist: Writings by the Opponents of the Constitution* (Chicago: University of Chicago Press, 1985), 80. See also Arkes, *Beyond the Constitution,* 59.

38. Storing, *What the Anti-Federalists Were For*, 67. See also Edmund Morgan, *Inventing the People: The Rise of Popular Sovereignty in England and America* (New York: Norton, 1988), chapter 11.

39. Madison, *National Gazette*, January 19, 1792, in ed. Padaver, *The Complete Madison*, 335.

40. Hamilton, *The Federalist Papers* 84, 513.

41. Hamilton, *The Federalist Papers* 84, 515.

42. See Wood, *The Creation of the American Republic*, 536–43.

43. See Harris, *The Interpretable Constitution*, 95.

44. Hamilton, *The Federalist Papers* 9, 74.

45. Hamilton, *The Federalist Papers* 84, 514.

46. Madison, *The Federalist Papers* 57, 353.

47. In *Beyond the Constitution*, Hadley Arkes develops a similar argument. He further suggests how contemporary debates over free speech, racial prejudice, religious pluralism, and abortion reflect the success of the Anti-Federalists' reliance on the provisions of the Bill of Rights. My focus on maintaining a capacity for deliberation is not offered as a full-fledged theory of rights. Nor do I mean to slight the Bill of Rights's role in protecting minorities. I share Arkes's concern that the Anti-Federalists' view of politics has undermined our ability to fully explore the nature of rights. My purpose, however, is to connect Publius's understanding of ''reflection and choice'' to a conception of peoplehood and the formation of citizens.

48. Alexis de Tocqueville, *Democracy in America* (New York: Vintage Books, 1945), vol. 1, 273.

49. Bradley Kent Carter and Joseph F. Kobylka, ''The Dialogic Community: Education, Leadership, and Participation in James Madison's Thought,'' *The Review of Politics* (1990/1): 54. (Emphasis in the original.) Also see p. 46.

50. In a letter written in 1829 Madison argued that ''the doctrine of the present day in South Carolina asserts that in a case of not greater magnitude than the degree of inequality in the operation of a tariff in favor of manufactures, she may of herself decide, by virtue of her sovereignty, that the Constitution has been violated; and that if not yielded to by the Federal government, tho' supported by all the other states, she may rightfully resist it and withdraw herself from the Union.'' Hunt, ed., *The Writings of James Madison*, vol. 9, 343–44. See Carter and Kobylka, ''The Dialogic Community,'' 54.

51. Stephen Elkin, *City and Regime in the American Republic* (Chicago: University of Chicago Press, 1987), 151.

Chapter Four

52. Sotirios A. Barber, *On What the Constitution Means* (Baltimore, Md.: Johns Hopkins University Press, 1984), 35–36.

53. See Sanford Levinson, *Constitutional Faith* (Princeton, N.J.: Princeton University Press, 1988), 139–42.

54. Madison, *The Federalist Papers* 37, 229. "When the Almighty himself condescends to address mankind in their own language, his meaning, luminous as it must be, is rendered dim and doubtful by the cloudy medium through which it is communicated."

55. Madison, *The Federalist Papers* 37, 230.

5

Reflections on Citizenship and Diversity

by Nathan Glazer

I begin with two stories about American citizenship in an age of diversity.

The first is from Ronald Takaki, third-generation Japanese American, a professor of ethnic studies at the University of California in Berkeley, and the writer of major books on the history of American attitudes and practices in dealing with minorities. He reports on a personal experience that has happened to him more than once: He will enter a taxi on his way to a college to give a lecture, and the taxi driver will ask, "And when did you come to this country?"

Other Asian Americans, native-born, without accents, will tell the same story, about the same question asked in similar circumstances. There is no need in this story to assume there is any hostility in asking the question: It may be asked in all friendliness. Perhaps we could embellish the story and the irony by adding that the taxi driver may himself be a first-generation immigrant, perhaps from Russia or Israel, speaking with an accent. I have read similar accounts a number of times in the weekly dealing with Asian-American affairs, *Asian Week*, generally told by a second- or third-generation Japanese American. The great majority of Japanese Americans are native-born, of second- or later generations. This does not prevent them from being ordinarily identified as recent newcomers, as indeed the majority of Asian Americans (but not Japanese Americans) are. And the point of the story is, how long does it take for a nonwhite to become accepted as an American, of the same quality and commitment as any American of European origin?

I have written "nonwhite," but that is not quite correct. No black need be concerned about being so addressed, unless he was speaking with a foreign accent! And, as we know, blacks from Haiti or Nigeria or other places will often stick to the foreign or African accent or to Spanish or French in order to indicate they are foreigners rather than native American blacks. And yet another aspect of the story: the foreign-born taxi driver, if he is white, will automatically assume, in asking the question, that he is closer to the America norm, because he is white and European, than the Asian American.

Which only underlines the point of the story: Something more seems to be needed, aside from native birth, no accent, and presumed American citizenship, to be considered by a stranger a full American. The formal and informal indications of full citizenship and membership are insufficient.

I

The second story is by Glenn Loury, reporting on a trip to Australia:

> On a recent visit to Australia I spent some time with a group of economists and sociologists at the local Bureau of Immigration and Multicultural Research. They were eager to explain to a visiting American how well their country was managing its immigration policy. They stressed two main goals: to encourage newcomers to seek Australian citizenship and to promote the idea of a multicultural identity so that these new citizens would not feel it necessary to abandon their cultural heritage as the price of adopting a new nation. What struck me about this policy was its seeming incoherence. In what precisely did these analysts imagine Australian national identity to consist? Why would anyone feel loyalty to a country that required so little of him in order to join it?[1]

This account can be supplemented with similar ones that lead one to wonder about the distinctive character of American citizenship. At a conference on multiculturalism in Canada, a Canadian academic told me about her experience in attending an American school in her teenage years. She was surprised by the emphasis on Americanization. I assume this meant the reciting of the Pledge of Allegiance, the singing of the national anthem, the celebratory character of the account of American history and the American political system in the appropriate courses in the public schools. She knew of no similar emphasis on Canadianization in the Canadian public schools she attended. In effect she joins Loury in asking, but from the other side, why there is such a substantial difference in what is expected or demanded from the person becoming a full member of the national community, between the public schools in Canada and the United States.

A rather different orientation to full membership in the national community seems to separate the major English-speaking countries of immigration, Canada, Australia, and the United States: We do considerably more in adding a distinctive content to the purely formal requirements for citizenship. We do it in the public schools, our chief formal institution for molding Americans. (At least, we used to do it in the public schools: with the rise of multiculturalism, how much we still do it is questionable, something that requires researching). We do it in our requirements for citizenship, as Loury suggested. Thus to become an American citizen one must know English, one must demonstrate knowledge of the Constitution and American political institutions. The Immigration and Naturalization Service publishes books and pamphlets, at various levels of sophistication and difficulty, on the Constitution and American history to assist the intending citizen in becoming sufficiently knowledgeable about these matters to pass a required examination. There is also required of the new citizen a rather formidable oath, to bear arms in the defense of his adopted country (women and citizens of whatever age take this oath) and to forswear allegiance to any other ''potentates and powers.'' It is a rather more awesome ceremony in adopting a new national identity than our fellow-countries of major immigration demand.

Perhaps more effective than either public schools or citizenship requirements in making new Americans is the common culture, of television, professional sports, movies, talk shows, celebrities, and the like. (The way one could detect a ''real'' American, as against a Nazi spy, in some World War II movies, was to question the suspicious character about baseball). We cannot be happy about what kind of American is shaped by this common popular culture, but, at the least, politics and some glimmerings of knowledge of how the political system works are part of it. After all, late-night comedians do make jokes based on current politics.

Despite these requirements, acquiring formal citizenship in the United States is hardly a daunting enterprise, contrasted with what is required in such European nations as Germany or France, which still have, formally or in the unformulated informal consciousness, requirements that the new citizen should be close to what is still conceived of as the organic nation, whose origins go back into the mists of a somewhat mythical past. We do not require any of this. Our origins are clearly recalled, taught, documented. A strong accent, a distant culture, is no bar to citizenship, although it is clear that whatever we mean by the American nation, the new citizen may not yet be considered a full member of it by many of his fellow citizens, because of race or accent.

II

The point of the two stories is to indicate two central paradoxes about American citizenship. On the one hand, it is open to all: we celebráte our multifarious origins and our openness in the museum of immigration on Ellis Island, in the Statue of Liberty, and in the formal pronouncements of presidents. On the other hand, compared to other countries of immigration, we demand more, a rather more extensive change of heart and identity than these other nations demand or expect. And the second paradox: Many of us, perhaps most of us, have a mind-set in which certain races and nationalities, despite their formal equality in American law, despite the fact that distinctions of race are not recognized in immigration or naturalization law, have a greater claim to becoming American and are accepted as more legitimately American than others.

From a historical point of view, we might argue there are no paradoxes, only a progression from a more exclusive sense of who can become an American to a more inclusive one. This is one of the key themes of Michael Lind's *The Next American Nation*.[2] He sees a progression from Anglo-America, to Euro-America, to Multicultural America. (I would put the progression somewhat differently because, if the issue is inclusion and the steady expansion of who—defined by race, religion, ethnicity—may be legitimately included, one should call the Third America more properly Universal America, as the terms of inclusion, set by the Civil Rights Act of 1964 and Immigration Act of 1965, did not imply anything about multiculturalism, as presently understood.) Despite whatever has happened to the Whig interpretation of history elsewhere, we can properly claim here progress as well as a progression. We can celebrate the ever-expanding notion of the American, in law as well as popular consciousness, to the point where that notion potentially encompasses the entire world and all its peoples, without restriction of race or religion or national origin. And so a Muslim cleric can open sessions of Congress today as legitimately as a Protestant minister. In the beginning, it is true, it could only be a Protestant minister of some denomination who could pronounce these opening prayers: but in time he has been joined, indicating the progressive widening of the idea of the American, by Catholic priests, Jewish rabbis, Eastern Orthodox priests. Undoubtedly Buddhist and Hindu clerics have already officiated.

We can also trace this progression in the formal laws controlling naturalization. The progression here has not been even and steady toward greater inclusiveness. There has been backsliding toward suspicion and strictness, but over time we can see a generally forward movement toward increasing openness. The very first federal naturalization law in 1790 required that an applicant be a ''free white person.'' Slavery still flourished, even if under some restriction in Northern states. This restriction to ''whites'' is nevertheless odd—did any nonwhites apply for naturalization at the time? Those who have recorded this history do not report so. But only two years of residence was required in the United States for citizenship. The Federalists, suspicious of the support new immigrants gave to Jeffersonians, increased the retired term of residence in the United States to fourteen years in 1795, but when the Republicans came to power with Jefferson in 1801, they set the term at five years, and it has basically stayed at that figure through many changes in law since.

The white restriction has had a curious history.

> During congressional debate on a revised naturalization law in 1870, Senator Charles Sumner of Massachusetts, a leading supporter of Reconstruction, proposed an amendment that would open naturalization to nonwhite as well as white aliens, but the measure was vehemently opposed by the western states, who were by that time intent on excluding alien Chinese from citizenship. Sumner invoked the Declaration of Independence in a Fourth of July oration to argue, ''It is 'all men' and not a race or color that are placed under the protection of the Declaration. . . . The word 'white,' wherever it appears as a limitation of rights, must disappear. . . .

Although Sumner lost in the Senate, shortly thereafter Congress made aliens of African descent or nativity eligible for naturalization. ''Under that law, Arabs and Hindus from Africa, but not necessarily from Asia, could qualify for citizenship.''[3]

Reed Ueda, whose account we follow, describes the tortured history of the limitation of naturalization to ''free whites'' and Africans or persons of African descent, and the ambiguous position in which this placed Asians. Chinese were excluded from immigration in 1882, yet many were in fact naturalized, and of course their children were citizens under the Fourteenth Amendment, which granted citizenship to all those born in the United States. Mexicans were also placed in an ambiguous status. They were after all brown, not white. A U.S. district court in Texas ruled that despite the fact that they were neither white nor black they could be naturalized under the constitution of the (former) Republic of Texas and laws and treaties affecting it when Texas became part of the United States.

In 1911, the situation was formalized by the new Bureau of Immigration and Naturalization: clerks were ordered to "reject declarations from aliens who were neither white persons nor persons of African birth and descent." This ruling did not really settle the matter, and all through the 1920s we find cases that would now seem fantastic to us and that reflect a society as fanatically committed to policing racial boundaries as apartheid South Africa: the cases among many others of an Arab from Western India claiming his forebears had not intermarried with Indians, an Armenian who quoted Herodotus to defend himself from the charge of being Asian, and a high-caste Hindu arguing his background was the same as that of eligible Europeans.

In World War I, during its aftermath, and in World War II, political restrictions on both the right of entry and citizenship expanded, but these were based on political opinions and activities. And yet race and ethnicity played a role. Jewish refugees were undoubtedly excluded during Hitler's war against the Jews because they were Jewish, and in World War II Japanese Americans, citizen and noncitizen alike, were interned simply because they were Japanese. Italians and Germans, whether citizens or aliens, were not so treated. But after World War II, the racial restrictions and distinctions in American law were rapidly reduced.

Although the political bases for exclusion or denial of citizenship expanded as a result of the Cold War, the racial limitations on citizenship were swept away in the McCarran-Walter Act of 1952. "At one stroke the arbitrary category of 'aliens ineligible for citizenship,' which had consigned Asian nationalities to the inferior status of permanent-resident aliens for nearly a century, was swept away." Ueda concludes his authoritative account of the history of American naturalization optimistically:

> By the mid-20th century the racial restrictions on naturalization seemed both impolitic and impractical. Experience had shown that all ethnic groups, given time and encouragement, had the capacity to assimilate into the national civic culture, and so U. S. citizenship was opened to all. . . . Fears that ethnocultural or racial background could inhibit the proper exercise of citizenship rights were supplanted by a confidence that citizenship was a transcendent status obtainable by all individuals who shared a common membership in a democratic polity.[4]

In the mid 1970s, few would have challenged this notion of the course of American citizenship, ever expanding from its original limitations to include people of whatever race, religion, national origin. That's what American history told us, and no one dreamed there could be any regress from the high points of the Civil Rights Acts and Immigration Act of 1964 and 1965, which wiped out all references to race and nationality in American law, and brought into being finally, as the Civil War amendments had promised a hundred years earlier, a full equality without distinction of race and color—and, as the new legislation of the mid-1960s also added, without distinction of religion or sex.

That was law. Common practice might still be different, and whites, Christians, or Protestants might be favored in many areas of life, as they could not be favored in law. But how long would that last in the face of the legal changes and the powerful agencies—some newly brought into existence—to police them? Legal equality would be followed by real equality. This was the period when, for example, anti-Semitism rapidly declined, the last barriers to Jewish advancement were being broken, and Jews would shortly be appointed as CEOs of major corporations and presidents of major universities, positions in which they had not been found as late as the 1960s. This was also the period in which expressions of prejudice and practices of discrimination against blacks also were rapidly declining. The anti-Japanese sentiment of World War II, the anti-Asian sentiments endemic in America since the mid-nineteenth century, were also in rapid decline. One could be optimistic that the last barriers to difference in treatment based on race, religion, nationality, were being swept aside. This was the point of view I expressed in a book of 1975, *Affirmative Discrimination.*[5] Within that circle of change and expectation, the book criticized affirmative action in employment, then still in its first few years of development, as well as busing for racial integration in schools and housing policies that required efforts to achieve a target racial mix in housing. All these were unnecessary in view of what was happening in American attitudes and transgressed the spirit of the Civil Rights Law of 1964, as well as its specific language and the specific promises of its sponsors that the law demanded only color-blind policies from government and employers. The first chapter of the book laid out the basis for this criticism of the new race-conscious policies by arguing that the spirit of our American Revolution and our founding documents and the civilization created on the North American continent aimed at this ultimate color-blindness, whatever the practical limitations that hindered the fulfillment of this aim for two centuries.

When Jefferson wrote, as a self-evident truth, "all men are created equal," slavery existed, there was discrimination against Jews and Catholics, and had there been any Asians or Hispanics around at the time there would undoubtedly have been discrimination against them too. But I asserted, with more boldness and self-confidence than I would today, that the spirit of our culture and polity made all these anomalies that would in time be eliminated. The pattern of American history steadily moved us to a more expansive notion of the American, finally fulfilled in the 1964 and 1965 civil rights and immigration legislation eliminating any consideration by government of race or religion or national origin. For this reason the rise of affirmative action in employment, in busing for school integration, and in racial targets for housing developments was a regression.

But what does one mean when one makes such claims for "the spirit of our culture," "the pattern of our history"? Who can pronounce on those with confidence? In *Affirmative Discrimination,* I drew on some leading authorities writing in the late 1950s and early 1960s on the development of American nationality and American national ideals: Seymour Martin Lipset in his *The First New Nation*, Hans Kohn and his *American Nationalism: An Interpretive Essay*, and Yehoshua Arieli and his *Individualism and Nationalism in American Ideology*.[6] All were quite confident that the pattern of American history showed this tendency toward greater inclusion and equality from its origins, and that the facts that demonstrated things were otherwise were anomalies that would in time be swept away by the implicit pattern, as they indeed had been.

These days, critics of this argument would probably note, if they were unkind enough, that my three chief authorities were the child of an immigrant, a refugee, and an Israeli, all Jews, who understandably would take this generous view of the course and aims of American history. It was not long after the publication of *Affirmative Discrimination* that Ronald Takaki, with whose personal account I began this essay, strongly attacked this optimistic view of the pattern and direction of American history in its treatment of the foreigner, the nonwhite, the other, as it is now put. And he had plenty of quotations from founding fathers to set against the ones that Lipset, Kohn, and Arieli—and I, following them—had recorded to defend our optimistic views regarding the inclusion of the nonwhite and the non-European into American society and polity.[7]

It seemed there could be very wide divergences as to how to interpret the pattern of American history and American attitudes and practices when it came to the incorporation of those outside the ethnic, linguistic, and racial circle of the original founders. Originally this divergence was surprising to me and to the main body of interpreters of American history and society. Who could dispute in 1965, or even in 1975, the viewpoint that the Civil Rights Acts and Immigration Act of 1964 and l965 represented a permanent advance to full inclusiveness? That challenge became easier and easier to make over time, climaxing in the debate over multiculturalism, in which the celebratory version of the story of the American people was denounced as simply the imposition of a Eurocentric view. The terms of the incorporation were challenged; assimilation as a desirable goal was challenged. Some of the racial and ethnic groups that made up America, it was charged, would never be fully included in the Euro-American version of our history and society, nor did they desire it. Various spokesmen for non-European races and ethnic groups demanded that both the story of their grievances and a full measure of respect and recognition should become part of the fundamental public school education that had incorporated and assimilated new elements in American society in the past.

In 1990 I was serving on a New York State committee to review the social studies curricula for the state. It was a committee that had been set up to repair the damage created by an earlier committee, which had, under the influence of the now notorious professor of black studies of the City College of New York, Leonard Jeffries, vigorously denounced social studies education as oppressive and Eurocentric and had called in effect for separate and equal curricula for blacks, Latinos, Asians, and Native Americans (American Indians). This report in turn had been denounced by a committee of leading historians, among them Arthur Schlesinger, Jr. and Diane Ravitch. Our committee, which included scholars, teachers, and administrators, strove to find a common basis for social studies education. In searching for an appropriate broad-based and general statement to introduce our recommendations, I came across a statement in a report by the Curriculum Task Force of the National Commission on Social Studies in the Schools, composed of leading historians and teachers of social studies, which seemed to me sound and unobjectionable. It read as follows:

> Classrooms today bring together young people of many backgrounds with a broad spectrum of life experience. We can expect an even more diverse student population in the twenty-first century. This diversity enriches our nation even as it presents a new challenge to develop social studies education that integrates all students into our system of democratic government

and helps them subscribe to the values from our past—especially our devotion to democratic values and procedures.

The coexistence of increasing diversity and cherished tradition require social studies in our schools to cultivate participatory citizenship. . . . The study of social involvement and often competing loyalties addresses basic questions: "Who am I?" "To what communities do I belong?" "What does citizenship in our nation require of me as an individual and as a member of the various groups to which I belong?"[8]

I will admit astonishment when the co-chairman of our small committee of two that had been assigned the task of writing the introductory statement for our report, an anthropologist who was an immigrant from Mexico, vigorously objected to the use of these to me unobjectionable and bland statements. He asserted that they suggested that "there is a fund of common values in the U.S. that should be imposed on all immigrants." He thought the contrast of "increasing diversity" and "cherished traditions" "uncharitable." He felt the use of the word "ours" was exclusionary. He saw in the statement the "xenophobic language of the nativists and the Americanization movement," of the "worst moments of U. S. chauvinism." He objected that the reference to "competing loyalties" deprecated the significance of group distinctiveness and group loyalty for minority groups. I interpret this objection to mean that he refused to place subgroup loyalty on the same level as a larger American loyalty: subgroup loyalty rather trumped American loyalty. He feared the "retreat of the Euro-American minority [the reference is to the time when the non-Europeans will become a majority] from the cherished guarantees found in the Constitution."

III

It is clear that today the triumphalist view of the history of American inclusion will not receive universal acceptance. We cannot settle the matter simply by reference to historical truth. Of course, there is the Declaration of Independence, but there is also slavery and the limitation of naturalization to whites (and blacks) for 150 years. And at every point in the history, the broadly inclusionary view can be contrasted with a narrow racist and chauvinist view. Which is to be dubbed the "mainstream" of American history? I know how I would judge the matter, and I believe history supports me, but I don't think I would convince the Japanese-American historian or the Mexican-American anthropologist with whom I have tussled on this matter. They would have a good deal of history and current practice on their side. Nor is it clear we even share a common objective. "Assimilation" was once such a common objective. It could mean many things, and, if one thing it means is equal treatment, then my opponents would agree it is a good thing. But another thing assimilation means is changing one's identity. And the reality that demonstrates that the identity does change and the immigrant does become an American would be seen as neither inevitable nor desirable.[9] Americanization is as unpopular these days as an objective for immigrants intending to become part of this nation as assimilation. What does all this do to our notion of American citizenship, which, I argued at the beginning, does come with a certain specific content and is more than a formal membership?

Some strange things have been happening in regard to citizenship in the last two decades that place both my view of 1975 and those of my critics in a new light. Those elements of the citizenship process that would surprise a Canadian or an Australian, that insist that becoming an American has a specific content, such as the requirement that one accept American political institutions, know the English language, renounce previous allegiances, have all been reduced over time in their weight and significance. They are still there, of course. But one may note that the demand for English (relaxed for the elderly who have been here a long time) does not prevent the existence of a Voting Rights Act that simultaneously imposes on local jurisdiction the requirement to facilitate the voting of those citizens who do not know English by, for example, requiring the translating of all propositions and the like into Spanish or Chinese or other protected languages. One may note that great numbers become citizens as a result of being born on American soil, despite the fact that their parents are neither citizens nor legal residents, and in effect are here in violation of law. Of course as citizens on grounds of birth nothing will be demanded of them as to language, beliefs, or allegiance. *Citizenship without Consent* is the provocative title of Peter Schuck and Rogers M. Smith's book about this anomaly. These newborns have become citizens without the consent of the citizen-body, nor, obviously, their own consent, which is required from applicants for citizenship.[10]

Just as demands we make on the prospective citizen have been reduced and the boundary we set to make citizenship a significant event has become less sharply defined, so simultaneously we have reduced the benefits that citizenship status offers as against the status of noncitizen immigrant. Affirmative action requirements seem to make no distinction between citizens and noncitizens. And the great majority of immigrants today are eligible for some degree of affirmative action. As Schuck and Smith point out, the growth of the welfare state means there are many benefits to being an American, benefits that were almost completely absent before the 1940s, and expanded greatly in the l960s and 1970s. But most of those benefits come whether one is a citizen or an immigrant, and indeed some public benefits (for example, free public education) are available even if one is an illegal immigrant child. In their l985 book, Schuck and Smith noted that even while the welfare state and its benefits were expanding, the courts were striking down distinctions between citizen and noncitizen that restricted benefits to citizens. It was all part of the great expansion of rights by court decisions in the period of the 1960s and l970s:

> [A] line of judicial decisions significantly lowered the political and economic value of citizenship by prohibiting government, especially the states, from allocating certain legal rights and economic advantages on the basis of that status. In the most important of these decisions, *Graham vs. Richardson* [1971], the Supreme Court invalidated statutes that restricted welfare benefits to United States citizens and legal residents who had resided in the United States for fifteen years. The Court held that alienage was a constitiutionally "suspect classification," one that could not ordinarily be used as a basis for allocating state-created advantages between citizens and aliens.
>
>   . . . [I]ts principle has been extended to invalidate citizenship requirements for some, but not all, professions and occupations regulated by state law. It has been held inapplicable to citizenship requirements for federally created entitlements, such as Medicare, and for federal civil service jobs. Even as qualified and limited by later cases, however, *Graham*'s repudiation of citizenship as a criterion for allocating the welfare state's "new property" entitlements is significant. Both in its radical departure from earlier case law on the validity of alienage classifications and in its refusal to regard citizenship as a special status entitling its holder to special advantages in the welfare state, *Graham* marks an important milestone in the devaluation of citizenship.[11]

Thus developments in the law have made it harder to limit public benefits or posts to citizens. Indeed our Constitution does refer more often to "persons" in specifying rights than to citizens or legal residents.

But 1995 marks a surprising turn in these developments, which have suddenly given increased value to legal residency and indeed to citizenship. California's Proposition 187, limiting public benefits to legal residents and citizens, adopted by the citizens of the state with the largest number of illegal (and legal) immigrants, has been challenged in the courts. What its fate will be is still unclear, and we may be seeing a reversal in the crescive process in which the value of citizenship has been steadily depreciated. There may be similar moves in other states. And in Congress, there are proposals, not yet law, to restrict some welfare benefits which are now available to all citizens, so as to exclude not only illegal immigrants but also legal immigrants, and in some cases naturalized citizens. This has led to a striking increase in the number applying for citizenship, and, for example, to much uncertainty over what education benefits (e.g., access to loans and grants) students who are formally illegal immigrants or even legal immigrants will be eligible for.[12]

IV

Where does that leave us in regard to the two paradoxes of citizenship and diversity with which I began? Those who have always been suspicious of the good faith of America in welcoming others—such as Ronald Takaki—will only have their suspiciousness—indeed, for many, their fear—increased. It all looks too much like a new war against the immigrants, a new restrictionism, driven by an inherent and ineradicable racism. I believe such fears are exaggerated. The incorporation of nonwhites into American polity and society is secure. Our great problem is not with nonwhite immigrants or their descendants. It is with native blacks, who have never been fully incorporated into American society, and whose distance from all the others—not only whites, but Asians and Latinos—is unique. This is the great American problem. American racism once extended to other groups, Asians and Latinos. But that kind of racism has been radically reduced. It is reduced, too, in regard to blacks, but there remains a difference of significance that is still the most troubling aspect of American life. What is driving the restrictions on illegal immigrants and on legal immigrants is much more concerns over public spending than racist fears and antagonisms—though, of course, they do exist. Peter Brimelow has raised the question, But isn't America changing as a result of immigration—racially, ethnically? Shouldn't we be concerned? For the most part, conservatives have rejected his argument.[13]

But what now of the other paradox? Welcoming as we are, we demand something from the immigrant who means to become a citizen. Here we have seen a reduction during the 1960s and 1970s in what we demand. As our law and attitudes changed in regard to all kinds of boundaries—white versus black, male versus female, foreigner versus native, citizen versus noncitizen—we have become much more generally accepting of difference. And then we have seen a more recent counter-reaction, in which some of these boundaries may be restiffened, and most relevant for our discussion, the benefits of citizenship will be enhanced, while the penalties for not becoming a citizen will be increased.

A recent new citizen, who had lived in this country for more than thirty years as student and permanent resident, observed to me, why is it that Americans seem so insistent that you should become a citizen? They take it for granted that citizenship is the best thing, the right thing, for anyone living in this country, anyone coming to this country. Nor do they necessarily express this expectation in a friendly manner. An oddity indeed. One response to the recent surge in citizenship applications might have been concern—let's make it harder, why do we need all these new citizens? But, quite the contrary, the official response has been that we must accommodate all these people who want to become citizens, make it easier for them to get through the bureaucratic hoops. Immigration and Naturalization Service Commissioner Doris Meissner said she planned to ask Congress to double the amount of money the agency spends on naturalization. She has

> personally advocated an expanded naturalization program . . . , arguing that as a matter of policy and national interest the INS should encourage eligible legal immigrants to seek citizenship. . . . One plan to speed up the naturalization process that will be tested this spring allows educational institutions—such as community colleges—to take over a substantial portion of the face-to-face interviews that immigration officers must conduct with all immigrants applying for U.S. citizenship.

There have been different reasons over time why permanent residents have been pressed to become citizens. In World War I and its aftermath, it was because of fears over loyalty: This was the way one showed one was a good American. In the early days of the Cold War, there was a similar motivation with the heyday of the "I Am an American" ceremony to induct new citizens. Today loyalty seems a less pressing matter, and the immigrant is urged to become a citizen for reasons that seem obscure: It will clear up an ambiguous status. It is better for the immigrant, who then won't have to worry about welfare, health, and education benefits. But are those really the reasons why we want immigrants to become citizens? I don't think so.

Underlying all the different motivations is one rock-bottom belief held broadly by Americans, regardless of their political orientation: it is better to be an American, and anyone can become an American. The first was always true, the second has been true for the past 40 years and is not going to change. Put the two together and one has a commitment to the making of Americans, regardless of race and ethnicity and religion, that is now unchallengeable.

Notes

1. Glenn Loury, "Terms of Engagement," *National Review* (May 1, 1995), 80.
2. Michael Lind, *The Next American Nation: The New Nationalism and the Fourth American Revolution* (New York: Free Press, 1995).
3. Reed Ueda, "Naturalization and Citizenship," in *Harvard Encyclopedia of American Ethnic Groups*, ed. Stephen Thernstrom (Cambridge, Mass.: Harvard University Press, 1980), 739. The quotations and the account of the history of the laws affecting naturalization generally in these and further paragraphs are from this authoritative source.
4. Ibid., 748.
5. Nathan Glazer, *Affirmative Discrimination: Ethnic Inequality and Public Policy* (New York: Basic Books, 1975; and Cambridge, Mass.: Harvard University Press, 1987, with a new introduction).
6. Seymour Martin Lipset, *The First New Nation* (New York: Basic Books, 1963); Hans Kohn, *American Nationalism: An Interpretive Essay* New York: Macmillan, 1957); Yehoshua Arieli, *Individualism and Nationalism in American Ideology* (Cambridge, Mass.: Harvard University Press, 1964).
7. Ronald Takaki, "Reflections on Racial Patterns in America," 26–37, in Ronald Takaki, ed., *From Different Shores* (New York: Oxford University Press, 1987).
8. From *Charting a Course: Social Studies for the 21st Century*. Report of the Curriculum Task Force of the National Commission on Social Studies in the Schools (Washington, D.C.: The Commission, 1989), 1.
9. See Nathan Glazer, "Is Assimilation Dead?", *The Annals* (November 1993).
10. Peter H. Schuck and Rogers M. Smith, *Citizenship without Consent: Illegal Aliens in the American Polity* (New Haven, Conn.: Yale University Press, 1985).
11. Ibid., 107.
12. See Sam Howe Verhoven, "Legal Immigrants Seek Citizenship in Record Numbers," *New York Times*, 2 April 1995; Lena H. Sun, "INS Sees Surge in Citizenship Seekers," *Washington Post*, 12 April 1995; Tatiana M. With, "The Newer Americans: A rush for citizenship," *Boston Globe*, 30 April 1995;

Scott Jaschik, "House Plan to Overhaul Welfare Would Eliminate Federal Student Aid for Many Legal Immigrants," *Education Week*, 7 April 1995; Lynn Schnaiberg, "College-Bound: Undocumented Students on Uncertain Path, *Education Week*, 5 April 1995.

13. Peter Brimelow, *Alien Nation: Common Sense About America's Immigration Disaster* (New York: Random House, 1995); and see reviews in *National Review*, 1 May 1995, 76–80.

6

Dred Scott and African American Citizenship

by Randall Kennedy

A strange thing has happened to Roger B. Taney's infamous ruling of 1857 in *Dred Scott v Sandford*[1] that *all* blacks and their descendants, whether slave or free, are excluded from United States citizenship.[2] Widely condemned on moral grounds, it is now also widely accepted as a legally correct application of the pre-Civil War federal constitution. An outstanding example is a speech delivered by Justice Thurgood Marshall on May 6, 1987, near the height of the celebration of the Constitution's Bicentennial. In "Reflections on the Bicentennial of the United States Constitution,"[3] surely one of the most controversial addresses given by a sitting justice in recent times,[4] Justice Marshall relied heavily upon Taney's opinion in the course of chastising the festive tenor of the memorial events. Remarking that he did not find "the wisdom, foresight, and sense of justice exhibited by the Framers particularly profound,"[5] Marshall maintained that "the government they devised was defective from the start, requiring several amendments, a civil war, and momentous social transformation to attain the system of constitutional government, and its respect for the individual freedoms and human rights, that we hold as fundamental today."[6] Turning to the Constitution's preamble—"We the People of the United States, in Order to form a more perfect Union . . . do ordain and establish this Constitution for the United States of America"—Justice Marshall echoed Taney in asserting that the original intent of those words were "far too clear for any ameliorating construction."[7] Marshall then affirmatively quoted Taney's judgment that, from the viewpoint of the Framers, blacks "are not included, and were not intended to be included"[8] among those comprising the new nation created by the Constitution and that, therefore, neither they nor their descendants could ever be considered citizens of the United States by right of birth. Finally, Marshall endorsed Taney's rendition of the status of blacks in the eyes of the Founding Fathers. Referring to Taney's opinion in *Dred Scott*, Marshall stated that "nearly seven decades after the Constitutional Convention, the Supreme Court reaffirmed the prevailing opinion of the Framers regarding the rights of Negroes in America."[9] Although Justices Benjamin R. Curtis and John McLean wrote lengthy and detailed dissents that poked gaping holes in Taney's argument on African American citizenship—dissents that many observers have found convincing, Justice Marshall makes no mention of them or anything else that draws into question the legality, as opposed simply to the morality, of Taney's conclusions. To the contrary, Justice Marshall refers to Taney's opinion as if it was unambiguously authoritative, a merely candid report of how the Founding Fathers intentionally excluded blacks from the new American polity.

Why did Justice Marshall accord such credence to Taney's opinion in light of the dissents and subsequent historical research that largely affirms objections voiced by the dissenters?[10] Lack of knowledge is one possibility. Like many landmark documents, more people have heard about *Dred Scott* than have actually read it. Made up of nine opinions that take up 240 pages in the United States Reports, *Dred Scott* discourages close study. Moreover, as Sanford Levinson has shown (and decried), *Dred Scott*, despite its central importance, is often given only cursory attention in constitutional law surveys in American law schools.[11] It is possible, indeed likely, that the law clerk who drafted Justice Marshall's speech knew little about *Dred Scott* beyond a conventional, which is to say inadequate, understanding of its holdings and context.

Another possibility is that Justice Marshall was aware of the deficiencies in his fellow Marylander's infamous opinion but viewed them as beside the point. He might have believed, along with several scholars, that notwithstanding specific historical errors and weaknesses in argumentation, Taney was essentially correct when he maintained, that, at the founding of the nation, African Americans were seen as a group— what Madison termed "an unhappy species of population"[12]— fundamentally apart from and alien to the new people created by the Constitution.[13] Or, Marshall might have thought that, whether or not it was "correct" or controversial, Taney's opinion was widely perceived then and now as "the Opinion of the Court" and the law of the land and that dissents and commentaries were, as a practical matter, irrelevant.

Although it is true that only two justices—James M. Wayne and Peter V. Daniel—joined Taney's opinion on the citizenship issue, it is also true that his opinion was perceived as sufficiently authoritative to prompt friends of the Negro to press for a constitutional amendment after the Civil War to safely inter the chief justice's odious holding.

Yet another possibility, the one most likely to explain Justice Marshall's treatment of *Dred Scott*, is that when he gave his speech he perceived himself to be acting as a statesman and not a scholar. As a statesman, he sought to shame the Bicentennial's most exuberant, unreflective celebrants, to emphasize the rootedness of Negrophobic racism, and to reallocate credit for the most noble aspects of the United States from the Founding Fathers and other conventional idols in American civil religion (including the justices of the Supreme Court) to the lesser known people whose ''suffering, struggle, and sacrifice . . . has triumphed over much of what was wrong with the original [Constitution.]''[14] If these were his goals, they were advanced by crediting the historical accuracy of Taney's opinion, making it the unambiguous holding of *Dred Scott*, and emphasizing the influence and pervasiveness of the racial attitude that Taney displayed. As Bruce Ackerman observes, ''The very idea that the Court could declare that *free* black people were *forever* barred from American citizenship remains . . . an awful rebuke to our Constitution.''[15]

As a matter of history, however, the citizenship status of the African American under the Constitution of 1787 is more complicated than either Justice Marshall or Chief Justice Taney suggest. Both wrongly homogenize the antebellum African American community and misleadingly simplify its relationship to the state and federal governments. The root of the problem is that they both disregard the free black population.[16]

Both Justice Taney and Justice Marshall also wrongly suggest that the Founders clearly indicated who constituted citizens of the United States, who counted as one of ''We the People.'' But a salient feature of the Constitution of 1787 is that it contained no definition of citizenship.[17] Citizenship was not entirely ignored. The Framers expressly authorized Congress ''to establish an uniform rule of naturalization.''[18] The Framers also expressly referred to citizenship when they delineated who would have access to federal courts,[19] declared that ''The Citizens of each State shall be entitled to all Privileges and Immunities of Citizens in the several States,''[20] and stipulated requirements for national office.[21] But the Framers left virtually undefined indicia of citizenship itself.[22] The Framers did not say who comprised ''We the People.'' And they certainly did not expressly write, "We the *white* People." They put no racial boundary around the status of citizenship. They left the matter open.

Soon after ratification of the Constitution, however, racial boundaries were employed to exclude certain persons from the realm of citizenship. One of the earliest laws passed by the Congress limited naturalization to "free white persons."[23] Although the early leaders of the Republic desired and sought to attract immigrants from abroad, they only wanted those who were "white." Although this law barred the world's people of color from eligibility for United States citizenship, it did not address the legal status of colored peoples born in the United States and residing there, namely Indians and African Americans. In 1831, in *Cherokee Nation v Georgia*,[24] the Supreme Court indirectly addressed the status of Indians when it concluded that tribes were, in some sense, nations with which the president and Congress were obligated to deal as sovereign or semisovereign political bodies. Courts subsequently decided that because tribes constituted nations, individual members of tribes were aliens to the United States and, hence, not citizens of it;[25] prior to 1924, when Congress extended citizenship to all Indians,[26] the only ones allowed to attain citizenship were those covered by special statutes or treaty provisions.[27]

The question whether slaves were citizens never arose in a pointed fashion that commanded widespread attention for it was so widely assumed that, as human property, they were not a part of "We the People." After all, as James H. Kettner, the foremost student of antebellum citizenship writes, "property had no national character. It was neither alien nor citizen."[28] A question, however, that did command widespread attention and revealed the moral and political divisions that slavery either caused or exacerbated was whether free blacks should properly be deemed citizens of the United States. Although the *Dred Scott* decision is the most well-known official response to that question during the antebellum era, all of the major arguments bearing on African American citizenship articulated in that ruling were anticipated thirty-six years earlier as part of the bitter debate over the Missouri Compromise.[29]

In 1819, Congress sought to resolve heightening tensions between the (mostly) free Northern states and the solidly slave Southern states by fashioning a compromise under which Missouri would be admitted to the Union as a slave state, Maine would be admitted as a free state, and slavery would be prohibited from the remainder of the Louisiana Purchase territory north of Missouri's southern border. The urgency of the felt need for this compromise is perhaps best recalled by remembering that Thomas Jefferson compared the Missouri controversy to "a fire bell in the night" that had awakened him and filled him with terror.[30] He felt such alarm because, as Glover Moore observes, the struggle over the admission of Missouri "was an epitome of the entire sectional controversy before 1860, containing all of the important elements of previous and future antagonisms. . . . [I]ts clarifying effects were not only great but appalling, and it was these which startled thoughtful men."[31]

Given the significance of the struggle over Missouri, it is noteworthy that one of the questions that came close to undoing the compromise was whether free blacks are citizens of the United States. The question arose because on the eve of its attainment of statehood, Missouri adopted provisions in its constitution that conferred upon the General Assembly the duty "as soon as may be, to pass such laws as may be necessary . . . to prevent free negroes and mulattos from coming to and settling in [Missouri] under any pretext whatsoever."[32] A number of United States senators and representatives strenuously objected to this provision. They pointed out that free blacks were considered to be citizens of at least certain states and had enjoyed that status at the time of the formation of the United States.[33] They then maintained that as citizens in these states, free blacks were entitled to the federal constitutional protection that guaranteed to the citizens of each state "all privileges and immunities of citizens in the several states." This was the main point pressed, for instance, by Representative Rollin C. Mallary of Vermont:

> We have been asked, if other States are allowed to declare who may be their citizens, shall not Missouri be indulged in the same power. She would be entitled to equal privileges, but no more. The people of that territory may make citizens of whom they please, among themselves. For one, I have little disposition to interfere. But when they attempt to disfranchise those, who have been made the citizens of other States, it is a matter of very different import. . . . The other States must then bow in submission. . . . Sir, no State in the Union would presume to deprive the citizens of Missouri of their rights, nor will they with composure allow [Missouri] a prerogative which they disavow for themselves.[34]

This response provoked, in turn, the heated rejoinder of congressional defenders of slavery who were acutely sympathetic to efforts to insulate enslaved blacks from the "mischievous example"[35] of free blacks enjoying at least the rudiments of basic liberties.[36] Intimating that the very idea of African Americans as United States citizens was a grotesque novelty, defenders of Missouri indignantly rejected the possibility. Representative Alexander Smith of Virginia argued, for instance, that "not every person who is born in a State and born free" could become "a member of the political community."[37] This position was based in part on an inference drawn from the logic of America's racist social order and in part on an appeal to the presumed original intent of the Founding Fathers, both of which were also central aspects of Chief Justice Taney's decision in *Dred Scott*. With respect to the first, the defenders of Missouri pointed to the humiliating racial distinctions imposed upon free blacks throughout the nation and reasoned that no group subject to such intense and widespread ostracism should properly be seen as a constituent element of the political community.[38] With respect to the second, the defenders of Missouri appealed in part to the memories of elder statesmen who had participated in the founding of the nation. Representative Charles Pinckney of South Carolina, who had served as a delegate to the Constitutional Convention of 1787, claimed now that he had actually authored the privileges and immunities clause, and insisted that he and his colleagues had never intended for blacks to be embraced with United States citizenship. "I say," he asserted, "that, at the time I drew that constitution, I perfectly knew that there did not then exist such a thing in the Union as a black or colored citizen, nor could I then have conceived it possible such a thing could ever have existed in it; nor, notwithstanding all that is said on the subject, do I now believe one does exist in it."[39]

The defenders of Missouri eventually maintained that the courts should settle the dispute. That did not happen, though it is tempting to speculate on what might have come of a suit adjudicated by the Supreme Court of John Marshall as opposed to the Supreme Court of Roger Taney. What did happen is that a compromise saved the Missouri Compromise. Congress voted the admission of Missouri pursuant to a resolution stating that the disputed provision of the Missouri constitution "shall never be construed to authorize the passage of any law . . . by which any citizen of either of the States in this Union shall be excluded from the enjoyment of any of the privileges and immunities to which such citizen is entitled under the Constitution of the United States."[40] Without deciding whether free African Americans could be citizens of the United States, the Congress stipulated that Missouri would be admitted on the condition that it avoid depriving citizens of federal constitutional rights. In other words, Congress "resolved" the question whether free African Americans are citizens of the United States by evading it.[41]

The question, however, did not go away. It arose again in the controversy over the Negro Seaman Acts. In 1822, after the discovery in Charleston that a plot to liberate the slaves had been organized by a free black, Denmark Vesey, South Carolina passed the Negro Seaman Act. Under this law, free black sailors aboard out-of-state or foreign ships calling to South Carolina ports were to be seized and imprisoned until their vessels were ready to depart. The law also provided that the ship's captain was to be financially responsible for paying the expenses of the imprisoned seaman's detention. If the captain defaulted on this responsibility, the prisoners would be sold into slavery. Other slave states followed South Carolina's example.

The seizure of an English black sailor prompted a suit that tested the constitutionality of South Carolina's statute. In *Elkison v Deliesseline*,[42] Supreme Court Justice William Johnson, sitting as a circuit judge, ruled in favor of the petitioner on the grounds that the law unconstitutionally infringed on the exclusive power of the federal government over interstate commerce and foreign affairs. Because the petitioner was a black Englishman, his case did not reach the questions whether a black American was a citizen of the United States entitled to the protection of the Constitution's comity clause and whether the South Carolina statute contradicted that entitlement. The case prompted reactions, however, that do illustrate the depth and intensity of the antebellum controversy over Negro federal citizenship, which Justice Taney tried mightily to make into a non-controversy.

Four reactions in particular are significant. First, the Georgia legislature implicitly conceded that free blacks were citizens of the United States by proposing to *amend* the federal Constitution so that it would read that "no part of the Constitution of the United States, ought to be construed, or shall be construed to authorize the importation or ingress of any person of color into any one of the United States, contrary to the laws of such state."[43] Second, the Senate of South Carolina promulgated a resolution that, as Andrew Kull observes, justified its Negro Seaman Act "on considerations transcending the issue of constitutionality":[44]

Resolved that it is as much the duty of the State, to guard against insubordination or insurrection among our colored population, or to control and regulate any cause which might excite or produce it, as to guard against any other evil, political or physical, which might assail us. This duty is paramount to all *laws*, all *treaties*, all *constitutions*:—it arises from the supreme and permanent law of nature, the law of self-preservation; and

will never by this state be renounced, compromised, controlled, or participated with any power whatever.[45]

A third reaction came from the North. In 1839 and 1842, the Massachusetts legislature passed resolutions protesting the imprisonment of
citizens of Massachusetts "without the allegation of the commission of
any crime, and solely on account of [their] color" and condemning such
detentions as "a gross violation of the federal constitution."[46] Soon,
Massachusetts passed additional resolutions of protest, and, moving beyond rhetoric, authorized the governor to appoint agents in various
Southern cities to bring lawsuits on behalf of Massachusetts citizens
"imprisoned without the allegation of any crime" so that the legality
of the Southern state's actions might be "tried and determined upon in
the supreme court of the United States."[47]

Massachusetts's actions prompted two rejoinders. Georgia, modify-
ing its previous interpretation of the comity clause, now insisted, echo-
ing the defenders of Missouri and anticipating Chief Justice Taney, that
"the term citizen, as used in [the Constitution], can only refer to those
who were embraced in its definition at the time of its adoption." On
that basis the Georgia legislature resolved that "negroes, or persons, of
color, are not citizens of the United States; and that Georgia will never
recognize such citizenship."[48] South Carolina responded with even
more militancy. First, no lawyer in the state was willing to serve as
an attorney for a detained seaman for the purpose of challenging the
legislation. Second, when Massachusetts sent a distinguished lawyer,
Samuel Hoar, to South Carolina, its legislature passed an act to punish
any person coming within the state with the intent to disturb the operation of laws relating to slaves and free persons of color and requested
the governor to expel him. Frightened by the very real possibility that
he would be subjected to mob violence, Hoar and his daughter departed
before he could initiate any litigation.[49]

Later, South Carolina's vision of federal-state relations would lead it
to secede from the Union, to fire on Union forces at Fort Sumter, and
thus to begin the American Civil War. In 1844, in the controversy over
the Negro Seamans Act, South Carolina's militant defense of state sovereignty had the smaller, but nonetheless important, effect of postpon-
ing once again an authoritative resolution of the question whether any
African American could properly be regarded a citizen of the United
States.

In 1857, Chief Justice Taney sought to provide a decisive resolution
of this question in the context of another dispute arising in Missouri. In

1834, a slave named Dred Scott was carried by his owner to the free state of Illinois and to the Wisconsin territory. Later, after he had been returned to Missouri, Scott sued for his freedom on the grounds that, under prevailing law, residence in free territory had transformed his legal status. In previous years he would almost undoubtedly have prevailed. By the 1850s, however, the Missouri authorities were hardening their defense of slavery against a rising tide of antislavery opinion in the free states. ''Times are not now as they were when the former decisions on this subject were made,'' declared Judge William Scott of the Missouri Supreme Court.[50] ''Since then,'' he continued:

> not only individuals but States have been possessed by a dark and fell spirit in relation to slavery, whose gratification is sought in the pursuit of measures, whose inevitable consequences must be the overthrow and destruction of our government. Under such circumstances it does not behoove the State of Missouri to show the least countenance of any measure which might gratify this spirit.[51]

After the state supreme court ruled against Scott, he brought suit again, this time against his new owner, John Sandford of New York, and this time in a federal court. Scott claimed to be entitled to invoke the federal court's jurisdiction under the provision of Article 3 of the Constitution, which endows such courts with ''Judicial Power'' to settle disputes ''between Citizens of different States''—so-called diversity jurisdiction. Dred Scott claimed that he was a citizen of Missouri suing a citizen of New York who was wrongfully enslaving him. The federal Circuit Court for the District of Missouri held that it had jurisdiction to adjudicate Scott's claim but then ruled against him on the merits of his suit, concluding that the Missouri Supreme Court's adjudication of his status was determinative.

At the U.S. Supreme Court, Chief Justice Taney held that the lower court erred in even hearing Scott's suit. According to Taney, Scott was not a ''citizen'' within the meaning of the federal Constitution even assuming that he was free. Because Scott was not a citizen of the United States, he lacked, in Taney's view, the capacity to invoke the limited jurisdiction of the federal courts.[52] To Taney, Scott's status as a slave or freeman did not matter for purposes of establishing whether he had a right to have access to the federal courts. To Taney, neither enslaved blacks nor free blacks nor any of their descendants could ever be citizens of the United States.[53] Free blacks could, he conceded, be citizens of their home states.[54] But he insisted that states did not have the author-

ity to endow blacks with federal citizenship on the basis of their status
as state citizens:

> It is very clear . . . that no State can, by any act or law of its own . . .
> introduce a new member into the political community created by the Con-
> stitution of the United States. It cannot make him a member of this com-
> munity by making him a member of its own. And for the same reason it
> cannot introduce any person, or any description of persons, who were not
> intended to be embraced in this new political family, which the Constitu-
> tion brought into existence, but were intended to be excluded from it.[55]

Taney's rhetoric and reasoning both echoed and supplemented that of
predecessors who had sought to preclude the possibility that African
Americans might be recognized as citizens of the United States of
America. He maintained that "every class and description of persons,
who were at the time of the adoption of the Constitution recognized as
citizens in the several States, became also citizens of the United
States," but declared that citizenship extended to none other. The nation, he asserted, "was formed by them, and for them and their posterity, but for no one else."[56] Therefore, he reasoned, "it becomes necessary . . . to determine who were citizens of the several States when
the Constitution was adopted."[57] Adverting to the political and social
condition of the thirteen colonies "when they separated from Great
Britain and formed new sovereignties," the racial character of those
who had declared their independence and "assumed the powers of Government to defend their rights by force of arms," and the language and
meaning of the Declaration of Independence and the Constitution,
Taney concluded that neither the African Americans of the Revolutionary Era "nor their descendants, whether they had become free or not,"
were recognized as members of the new American political family:

> It is difficult at this day to realize the state of public opinion in relation
> to that unfortunate race, which prevailed in the civilized and enlightened
> portions of the world at the time of the Declaration of Independence, and
> when the Constitution of the United States was framed and adopted. But
> the public history of every European nation displays it in a manner too
> plain to be mistaken.
>   They had for more than a century before been regarded as beings of an
> inferior order, and altogether unfit to associate with the white race, either
> in social or political relations; and so far inferior, that they had no rights
> which the white man was bound to respect; and that the negro might justly
> and lawfully be reduced to slavery for his benefit. . . . This opinion was at

that time fixed and universal in the civilized portion of the white race. It was regarded as an axiom in morals as well as in politics, which no one thought of disputing, or supposed to be open to dispute; and men in every grade and position in society daily and habitually acted upon it in their private pursuits, as well as in matters of public concern, without doubting for a moment the correctness of this opinion.[58]

Confronting the fact that the language of neither the Declaration of Independence nor the Constitution expressly referred to race, Taney reasoned that the Framers could not possibly have meant to include blacks—"beings so far inferior that they had no rights which the white man was bound to respect"[59]—within the bounds of citizenship defining the national family. For substantiation, he pointed to an ample record of antiblack ostracism—laws prohibiting transracial marriages, punishing blacks for striking whites, excluding blacks from militias, requiring segregation in schooling, and limiting United States citizenship through naturalization only to whites. These and other provisions demonstrated, Taney argued, that "a perpetual and impassable barrier was intended to be erected between the white race and the one which they had reduced to slavery."[60] Moreover, Taney remarked, the Framers of the Declaration of Independence and the Constitution of 1787 were "great men—high in literary accomplishments—high in their sense of honor, and incapable of asserting principles inconsistent with those upon which they were acting."[61] He thus concluded that "They perfectly understood the meaning of the language they used, and how it would be understood by others; and they knew that it would not in any part of the civilized world be supposed to embrace the negro race, which by common consent, had been excluded from civilized Governments and the family of nations, and doomed to slavery."[62]

Moving from an argument based on historical inference to an argument based on textual analysis, Taney maintained that "there are two clauses in the Constitution which point directly and specifically to the negro race as a separate class of persons, and show clearly that they were not regarded as a portion of the people or citizens of the Government then formed."[63] One was the slave-trade clause that prohibited Congress from interfering with the importation of slaves from abroad until 1808 and the other was the fugitive slave clause that provided that slaves would remain the property of their masters even if they escaped to "free" states or territories within the United States. According to Taney, these two provisions showed "conclusively" that neither slaves nor their descendants "were embraced in any of the other provisions of the Constitution; for certainly these two clauses were not intended to confer on them or their posterity the blessings of liberty, or any of the personal rights so carefully provided for the citizen."[64]

Finally, moving from an argument based on constitutional text to one based on constitutional structure, Taney maintained that free blacks could not be considered citizens of the United States because

> it cannot be believed that the large slaveholding States regarded them as included in the word citizens, or would have consented to a Constitution which might compel them to receive them in that character from another state. For if they were so received, and entitled to the privileges and immunities of citizens, it would exempt them from the operation of the special laws and from the police regulations which [the slaveholding class] considered to be necessary for their own safety. . . . It is impossible . . . to believe that the great men of the slaveholding States, who took so large a share in framing the Constitution of the United States, and exercised so much influence in procuring its adoption, could have been so forgetful or regardless of their own safety and the safety of those who trusted and confided in them.[65]

Taney's claims were vigorously rebutted by Justices John McLean and Benjamin Curtis. Curtis's dissent is particularly worthy of note for two reasons. First, it is the more elaborate and thorough of the two. Second, Curtis was the more conservative of the two justices. Contrasting his opinion with Taney's usefully underlines the point that belief that free blacks could be citizens of the United States was by no means a marginal idea embraced only by abolitionists. Curtis was a northern conservative Whig—a so-called Cotton Whig—who, as Kenneth Stampp observes, "considered the preservation of the Union worth any price—including respect for what [he] accepted as the constitutional rights of slaveholders."[66]

"It is not true," Justice Curtis declared, "that the Constitution was made exclusively by and for the white race."[67] Backing up this assertion, he notes in irrefutable detail that blacks were not only recognized as citizens of five of the original thirteen states (New Hampshire, Massachusetts, New York, New Jersey, and North Carolina) at the time of the Founding, but that in these states otherwise qualified blacks were eligible voters who likely had a say in ratifying the Constitution. In Curtis's words, "colored persons were not only included in the body of 'the people of the United States,' by whom the Constitution was ordained and established, but in at least five of the States they had the power to act, and doubtless did act, by their suffrages, upon the question of its adoption."[68] Curtis repeated and underlined this historical point, for it allowed him to hang Taney by his own originalist premises. Because, according to Taney, the boundaries of United States citizenship were to be determined by who was included in "We the People" as of 1787, it stood to reason, according to Curtis, that "as free colored persons were then citizens of at least five states, and so in every sense part of the people of the United States, they were among those for whom and whose posterity the Constitution was ordained and established."[69]

Taney spent considerable space in his opinion detailing the many ways in which state governments and the federal government discriminated against African Americans in terms of the franchise, military service, education, and other activities. His purpose was to suggest that no group so ostracized could plausibly have been intended as part of the republic's citizenry. Curtis noted, however, that the society was shot through with disabling legal discriminations against groups of persons who were deemed unquestionably to be citizens.[70] "Whether native-born women, or persons under age, or under guardianship because insane or spendthrifts, be excluded from voting or holding office, or allowed to do so, I apprehend no one will deny that they are citizens of the United States."[71] Turning to a discriminatory congressional statute that limited enrollment in the militia to only "free, able-bodied, white citizen[s]," Curtis remarked that "an assumption that none but white persons are citizens, would be as inconsistent with the just import of this language, as that all citizens are able-bodied, or males."[72] The truth of the matter, Curtis averred, "is that citizenship . . . is not dependent on the possession of any particular political or even civil rights."[73] That free blacks had been deprived of political and civil rights did not mean, therefore, that they were precluded from citizenship, a discrete status distinguishable from that of eligibility to vote or hold office or sit on a jury.

Taney claimed that the Founding Fathers would certainly have assumed that their audience would understand that the words of the nation's founding documents, although lacking any express reference to racial distinctions, implicitly carried a racial exclusion. Curtis suggested, by contrast, that the Constitution's Framers meant exactly what they had stated in 1776 and 1787. "It would not be just to them, nor true in itself, to allege," Curtis declared, that the Founding Fathers intended to say "that the Creator of all men had endowed the white race, exclusively, with the great natural rights."[74] The Founders, he maintained, "were ready and anxious to make effectual . . . the great truths they asserted."[75] But they were only willing to do so in light of "a necessary regard to circumstances, which no statesman can disregard without producing more evil than good.''[76] While Taney portrayed the Founding Fathers as men who assumed they were creating a republic for white people only, Curtis portrayed them as men committed to raceless, ''universal abstract truths,'' but devoted even more to recognizing the limits on idealism imposed by circumstance—the circumstance in this case being the need to acquiesce to slavery and its kindred institutions for the sake of creating and maintaining the unity of the United States.[77] Taney asserted that excluding blacks from the possibility of citizenship would certainly have been part of a statesmanlike concession to ''circumstances.'' But Curtis points out that Southern slaveholding representatives tried but *failed* to have the term ''white'' inserted into the privileges and immunities clause of the Articles of Confederation ''so that the privileges and immunities of general citizenship would be secured only to white persons.''[78] He further suggests that insofar as the Framers of the Constitution must have been aware of this earlier struggle and left the language of the clause unamended, it made sense to conclude that the Constitution's privileges and immunities clause applied to free persons of color who were citizens of the states in which they resided.

The point here is not to catalogue every aspect of the Taney-Curtis debate over African Americans' eligibility for federal citizenship. The point is to argue that Curtis's dissent persuasively challenges important aspects of Taney's analysis and that his efforts should not be permitted to become obscure.

Nor should contemporaneous condemnations of and resistance to Taney's opinion be allowed to be forgotten. Horace Greeley's *New York Tribune,* for instance, harshly castigated Taney's ruling, including his holding on African American citizenship, terming it ''atrocious,'' ''wicked,'' and ''abominable,'' a ''collation of false statements and shallow sophistries'' stitched together by a ''cunning chief.''[79]

African Americans were among those who condemned Taney's opinion. Some blacks, anticipating the stance adopted by Justice Marshall, condemned the morality of Taney's opinion but conceded its legality under what they viewed as an unequivocally pernicious, proslavery Constitution. That is the upshot of Robert Purvis's statement that *Dred Scott* ''furnishes final confirmation of the already well known fact that under the Constitution and Government of the United States, the colored people are nothing, and can be nothing but an alien, disfranchised, and degraded class.''[80] Other blacks, however, attacked the legality as well as the morality of Taney's judgment. One was yet another remarkable Marylander, the former slave Frederick Douglass. At an early stage in his career as an antiracist activist, Douglass, too, had preached wholesale rejectionism. Addressing a meeting of the American Anti-Slavery Society in 1847, he maintained:

> I have no patriotism. I have no country. . . . I cannot have any love for this country or for its Constitution. I desire to see it overthrown as speedily as possible, and its Constitution shivered in a thousand fragments.[81]

But later Douglass became a leading spokesman for abolitionists who interpreted the Constitution in a fashion that made it capable of accommodating not only African American citizenship but also the abolition of slavery. Condemning the *Dred Scott* decision as a "vile and shocking abomination,"[82] and charging especially that Taney "has grossly falsified history,"[83] Douglass asserted that "Washington and Jefferson, and Adams, and Jay, and Franklin, and Rush, and Hamilton, and a host of others, held no such degrading views . . . as are imparted by Judge Taney to the Fathers of the Republic.[84]

The Taney–Marshall portrayal of antebellum constitutional history—a portrait in which antiblack, proslavery racism is uniform, pervasive, unlimited, and thus wholly triumphant—fails to acknowledge too much that is important to recall. It fails to acknowledge that the Framers of the Constitution paid little attention to the boundaries defining eligibility for citizenship, that racial attitudes changed between the founding of the nation in 1787 and the country's radical polarization in the 1850s, that bitter fights erupted on several occasions over Dred Scott, that even many antiabolitionist, antiblack racists believed that free black citizens of a state should be deemed citizens of the United States.

The sordid tradition of proslavery constitutionalism that Chief Justice Taney exemplified is not excused by insisting that right alongside it existed other traditions more amenable to accepting, respecting and even nurturing the humanity, rights, and participation of African Americans and other peoples of color. This important countertradition included strains of racial egalitarianism that helped to prepare the ground for Reconstruction and that remain, to this day, on the leading edge of social thought.[85] Blacks in antebellum America glimpsed this countertradition and its capacity to supersede its ugly rival. This explains, in part, why, in 1827, in the opening editorial of the first black newspaper in the United States, the editors of *Freedom's Journal* declared that "in our discussion of political subjects we shall ever regard

Chapter Six

the Constitution of the United States as our political star.''[86] It also goes far to explain why William Howard Day, at the State Convention of Ohio Negroes in 1851 would be moved to declare:

> [C]oming as I do, in the midst of three millions of men in chains, and five hundred thousand only half free, I consider every instrument precious that guarantees to me liberty. I consider the Constitution the foundation of American liberties, and wrapping myself in the flag of the nation, I . . . plant myself upon the Constitution . . . and appeal to the American people for the rights thus guaranteed.[87]

The editors of *Freedom's Journal*, William Howard Day, Frederick Douglass, and many others who rejected Taney's distorted history and racist policy were neither naive nor simply making the best of a terrible situation. They perceived, realistically, a tradition in American constitutional thought and feeling that has periodically blossomed. One such blossom was Section One of the Fourteenth Amendment. That provision, for the first time, set forth a constitutional definition of citizenship—''[a]ll persons born . . . in the United States and subject to the jurisdiction thereof, are citizens of the United States.'' It established beyond question the birthright citizenship of African Americans. It buried the most odious aspect of *Dred Scott*. Even on this side of the constitutional divide, which the Fourteenth Amendment signifies, we should not forget that as a *legal* matter in the antebellum period, despite Taney's opinion, and even within the constraints imposed by the existence of slavery, free African American citizens of the various states should have been recognized as citizens of the United States. To forget or ignore or minimize that is to grant the most wicked Chief Justice in American history[88] a victory that we cannot afford and that he does not deserve.

Notes

1. 60 US (19 How) 393 (1857).
2. What was a binding ruling as distinct from mere *obiter dictum* has itself long been a subject of hot dispute. For a useful discussion of this issue, see Don E. Fehrenbacher, *The Dred Scott Case: Its Significance in American Law and Politics* (New York: Oxford University Press, 1978), 322–344. The Court is widely perceived to have also decided that Congress lacked constitutional authority to prohibit slavery in the territories, thereby invalidating the Missouri

Compromise. Fehrenbacher's volume is the most comprehensive available treatment of *Dred Scott.*

3. Hereinafter referred to in the notes as Marshall, ''Reflections,'' 101 *Harv L Rev* 1 (1987).

4. Compare William Bradford Reynolds, ''Another View: Our Magnificent Constitution,'' 40 *Vanderbilt L Rev* 1343 (1987) with Raymond T. Diamond, ''No Call to Glory: Thurgood Marshall's Thesis On the Intent of a Pro-slavery Constitution,'' 42 *Vanderbilt L Rev* 93 (1989). The Washington Legal Foundation suggested that Justice Marshall resign because his remarks ''reflect a deep-seated bitterness and dislike that impair his capacity.'' 102 *U.S. News & World Report,* 19 Sept. 1987, 12.

5. Marshall, ''Reflections,'' 2.

6. Ibid.

7. Ibid., 4.

8. Ibid.

9. Ibid.

10. See, e.g., Fehrenbacher, *The Dred Scott Case*, 335–64.

11. See Sanford Levinson, ''Slavery in the Canon of Constitutional Law,'' 68 *Chicago-Kent L Rev* 1087 (1993).

12. See *Federalist Papers,* No. 43.

13. William M. Wiecek writes, for instance:

> We condemn Chief Justice Roger B. Taney's statement [in *Dred Scott*] that blacks in 1787 ''had for more than a century before been regarded as beings of an inferior order, and altogether unfit to associate with the white race, either in social or political relations; and so far inferior that they had no rights which the white man was bound to respect.'' But we forget that his statement was a fair description of the constitutional world of 1787 at both the federal and state levels. Given the prevalent racism of the eighteenth century, we may no more expect the original Constitution to contain an implicit egalitarian promise than we may expect it to confer full political capacity on women.

William M. Wiecek, ''The Blessings of Liberty: Slavery in the American Constitutional Order,'' in *Slavery and Its Consequences: The Constitution, Equality, and Race*, ed. Robert A. Goldwin and Art Kaufman (Washington, D.C.: American Enterprise Institute for Public Policy Research, 1988) 28.

14. Marshall, ''Reflections,'' 5. At another point in his talk, Justice Marshall makes this point explicitly, noting that '' 'We the People' no longer enslave but the credit does not belong to the framers. It belongs to those who refused to acquiese in outdated notions of 'liberty,' 'justice,' and 'equality,' and who strived to better them.'' Ibid.

15. Bruce A. Ackerman, *We The People: Foundations,* vol. 1 (Cambridge, Mass.: Belknap Press of Harvard University Press, 1991) 63.

16. According to the 1790 census, there were 59,447 free blacks in the

United States and 697,624 slaves. According to the 1860 census, the population of the free blacks had risen to 488,070 and the population of slaves to 3,953,760. See Jessica Carney Smith & Carrell Peterson Horton, *Historical Statistics of Black America* (1818 [New York: Gale Research, 1995]).

17. See generally Alexander M. Bickel, "Citizenship in the American Constitution," 15 *Ariz L Rev* 369 (1973).

18. US Const, Art I, §8, cl 4.

19. US Const, Art III, §2.

20. US Const, Art IV, §2, cl 1.

21. US Const, Art I, §2 (prior to their installment, members of the House of Representatives must be citizens for seven years); US Const, Art I, §3 (senators must be citizens for nine years); US Const, Art II, §5 (the president must be "a natural born citizen, or a citizen of the United States at the time of the adoption of this Constitution"). The Constitution imposes no requirement of citizenship for federal judges.

22. Bickel, "Citizenship," 370 ("citizenship was nowhere defined in the original Constitution").

23. 1 Stat 103 (1790). See generally Charles Gordon, "The Racial Barrier to American Citizenship," 93 *University of Pennsylvania L Rev* 237 (1945); Ian Haney Lopez, *White by Law: The Legal Construction of Race* (forthcoming).

24. 30 US 1 (1831).

25. See generally James H. Kettner, *The Development of American Citizenship, 1608–1870* at 288–300 (Chapel Hill, N.C.: Published for the Institute of Early American History and Culture, 1978).

26. 43 Stat 253, codified as 8 USC §1401 (a) (2).

27. See Kettner, *The Development*, 297.

28. Ibid.

29. See generally Glover Moore, *The Missouri Controversy, 1819–1821* (Gloucester, Mass.: P. Smith, 1967).

30. Quoted in Fehrenbacher, *The Dred Scott Case*, 111.

31. Ibid., 342. Others besides Jefferson apprehended the implications of the Missouri controversy. John Quincy Adams called it the "title-page to a great tragic volume." Quoted in Moore, *The Missouri Controversy*, 339.

32. See Annals of Congress, 16th Cong., 2d sess., 47, Dec. 1820 (hereinafter referred to as Annals).

33. Representative William Eustis of Massachusetts declared, for instance, that in his state "the citizens in question constituted, and were in fact an elementary part of the Federal compact. They were as directly represented as the whites, in the initiatory process; and from their votes, in common with those of the whites, emanated the convention of Massachusetts, by whom the Federal Constitution was received and ratified." Annals, 637–38.

34. Ibid., 630.

35. The phrase comes from an opinion of the Mississippi Supreme Court alluding to the "danger" that the presence of free blacks posed to the slavery

regime. *Shaw v Brown,* 35 Miss 246, 320 (1858). For a useful, brief discussion of the constitutional issues that surrounded efforts taken by Southern slave states to quarantine themselves against the "contagion" of rebellion carried by free blacks, see Paul Finkelman, "State's Rights North and South in Antebellum America," 130–133, in *An Uncertain Tradition: Constitutionalism and the History of the South,* ed. Kermit L. Hall and James W. Ely, Jr. (Athens, Ga.: University of Georgia Press, 1989).

36. Even though some African Americans were free in antebellum America, North and South, everywhere they suffered from humiliating racial discriminations that limited or precluded their ability to sit on juries, vote, hold office, enjoy public accommodations, or pursue desired employment. See Leon Litwack, *North of Slavery: The Negro in the Free States, 1790–1860* (Chicago: University of Chicago Press, 1961); Paul Finkelman, "Prelude to the Fourteenth Amendment: Black Legal Rights in the Antebellum North," 17 *Rutgers LJ* 415 (1986); Ira Berlin, *Slaves without Masters: The Free Negro in the Antebellum South* (New York: New Press, 1974).

37. Annals, 556.

38. Ibid., 57–58. Articulating this point, Senator William Smith of South Carolina remarked:

Although they are not slaves themselves, who were prohibited by this constitution to settle in Missouri; yet they are the late offspring of slaves, and have been placed and considered in the body politic upon the same footing and no other . . . [the laws of the United States and the several states] furnish a mass of evidence, which nobody could doubt but a skeptic, that free negroes and mulattoes have never been considered as part of the body politic.

39. Ibid. 1134.

40. Moore, *The Missouri Controversy*, 155.

41. The author of this evasion was the speaker of the House of Representatives, Henry Clay, who won the title of "Great Pacificator" in part on the basis of his performance. See Moore, *The Missouri Controversy*, 159. One of Clay's colleagues wrote at the time "that Henry Clay of Kentucky saved that which George Washington of Virginia won—the United Independence of America." Quoted in Moore, *The Missouri Controversy.*

42. 8 Fed Cas 493 (CCSC 1823) (no. 4, 366).

43. S Res of 22 Dec 1823, 1823 Ga Acts 231.

44. Andrew Kull, *The Color-Blind Constitution* (Cambridge, Mass.: Harvard University Press, 1992), 12.

45. See S Res of 8 Dec 1824, reprinted at 27 Niles' Weekly Reg. 264 (25 Dec 1824).

46. Resolves of 3 March 1842, ch. 82, 1842 Mass Acts 568. See also Resolves of 8 April 1839, ch. 66, 1839 Mass. Acts 105.

47. Resolves of 24 March 1843, ch. 67, 1843 Mass. Acts 81. See also Resolve of 16 March 1844, ch. 111, 1844 Mass. Acts 330.

48. S Res of 24 December 1842 Ga Acts 181–82.
49. See generally Henry Wilson, *History of the Rise and Fall of the Slave Power in America,* 578–86 (New York: Negro University Press, 1872).
50. *Scott v Emerson,* 15 Missouri 576, 582 (1852).
51. Ibid., 582.
52. In addition to the citizenship issue, Taney's other major conclusion was that Congress lacked constitutional authority to bar slaveowners from taking slaves into federal territory. He invalidated, in other words, the Missouri Compromise and, further, appeared to condemn as constitutionally impermissible the program of the Republican Party.
53. See *Dred Scott,* 403: "Can a negro, whose ancestors were imported into this country, and sold as slaves, become a member of the political community formed and brought into existence by the Constitution of the United States, and as such become entitled to all the rights and privileges, and immunities, guaranteed by that instrument to the citizen?" A few sentences on, Taney returns to the subject to make it clear that he means to exclude from United States citizenship *all* African Americans including "the descendants of such slaves, when they shall be emancipated, or who are born of parents who had become free before their birth."
54. Ibid., 405: "[W]e must not confound the rights of citizenship which a State may confer within its own limits, and the rights of citizenship as a member of the Union. It does not by any means follow, because he has all the rights and privileges of a citizen of a State, that he must be a citizen of the United States. . . . The rights which he would acquire would be restricted to the State which gave them."
55. Ibid., 406.
56. Ibid.
57. Ibid., 407.
58. Ibid., 408.
59. Ibid., 407.
60. Ibid., 409.
61. Ibid., 410.
62. Ibid., 419.
63. Ibid., 411.
64. Ibid.
65. Ibid., 417.
66. See Kenneth Stampp, "Comment on Earl Maltz, The Unlikely Hero of Dred Scott," __ Cardozo LR __ (1995). See also Earl Maltz, "The Unlikely Hero of Dred Scott: Benjamin Robbins Curtis and the Constitutional Law of Slavery," __ Cardozo Law LR __ (1995).
67. *Dred Scott,* 582.
68. Ibid., 576.
69. Ibid., 582.
70. Ibid., 583.

71. Ibid.
72. Ibid., 587.
73. Ibid.
74. Ibid., 575.
75. Ibid.
76. Ibid., 76.
77. For a modern interpretation of the Founding Fathers that supports Curtis's portrayal, see William W. Freehling, ''The Founding Fathers and Slavery,'' in *American Negro Slavery: A Modern Reader*, ed. Allen Weinstein, Frank Otto Gatell, and David Sarasohn, 3d ed., (New York: Oxford University Press, 1979).
78. Freehling, *American Negro Slavery*, 575.
79. Quoted in Fehrenbacher, *The Dred Scott Case*, 417.
80. See Herbert Aptheker, *A Documentary History of the Negro People in the United States* (New York: Citadel Press, 1951), 392.
81. Quoted in R. Dick, *Black Protest: Issues and Tactics* (Westport, Conn.: Greenwood Press, 1974), 59.
82. John W. Blassingame, ed. 3 *The Frederick Douglass Papers: Series One: Speeches, Debates, and Interviews, 1855–63,* ed. (New Haven, Conn.: Yale University Press, 1985), 163.
83. Ibid., 180.
84. Ibid.
85. See Andrew Kull, *The Color-Blind Constitution.*
86. See Dick, *Black Protest*, 44 (quoting *Freedom's Journal,* 16 March 1827, at 1.)
87. Aptheker, *A Documentary History*, 318.
88. See Paul Finkelman, ''Hooted Down in the Page of History: Reconsidering the Greatness of Chief Justice Taney,'' *Journal of Supreme Court History* 83 (1994).

Index

abolitionism, 115
Ackerman, Bruce, 103
Act of Settlement (1689), 35
Adams, John, 53
Adams, John Quincy, 67, 118n. 31
affirmative action, xiii, 91, 92, 95–96
Affirmative Discrimination (Glazer),
    91, 92
African aliens, 89
African Americans, 71, 97; black
    aliens and, 86; British provocation
    of, 49; curricula for, 93; in 1960s,
    91. *See also* civil rights movement;
    free blacks; slaves
Agrippa (pseudonym), 69–70
Alford (Mass.), 50
Alien and Sedition Acts, 78
Alien residents, alienated residents
    and, 40n. 8; bar membership and,
    29–31, 32; illegal, 26, 95, 96;
    status of, 95–96; teaching by, 33;
    voting by, 42n. 30. *See also* immi-
    grants; minority groups
altruism, x; crises and, 6–7; human
    capacity for, 11–12; multinational
    enterprise and, 24; parental, 21;
    polity size and, 6; residence and,
    36; social reform and, 37. *See also*
    civic virtue
Ambach v Norwich, 33
American Anti-Slavery Society, 115
American Bar Association, 29, 33, 34,
    43n. 53

American Civil War, 23, 47, 51, 108
American Indians, 49, 69, 71, 93, 104
Americanization. *See* naturalization
American Nationalism (Kohn), 92
American Revolution, xii, 2, 45–61;
    Federalist on, 72; race question
    and, 91; republicanism from, 4
ancient republicanism. *See* classical
    republicanism
Anne Arundel County, 51
Anti-Federalists, 68–70; Bill of
    Rights and, xii, 69, 74, 83n. 46; pa-
    rochialism of, 78; Publius vs., 75,
    76–77; time sense of, 73
anti-pollution devices, 27, 28
anti-Semitism, 91, 92
anti-slavery movement, 115
apartheid, 90
Arabs, 89, 90
Argentina, 10
Arieli, Yehoshua, 92
aristocracy, 4, 5, 55
Aristotle, 2
Arkes, Hadley, 65, 83n. 46
Armenians, 90
Articles of Confederation, 68, 114
Ashby (Mass.), 46
Asian Americans, 85, 86, 93, 97
Asians, 89, 90, 91, 92
Asian Week (periodical), 85
assimilation, xiii, 93, 95
associations, 12, 63; in citizen forma-

loyalists, 51
loyalty, of business firms, 27; competition for, 21–22; constitutions and, 68; high levels of, 77; of immigrants, 98; legal advocacy and, 34, 35; Lieber on, 20; Pangle on, 67; to subgroups, 94
Luban, David, 43n. 55
Lukacs, Georg, 25, 26

McCarran-Walter Act (1952), 90
Macedo, Steven, 67
Machiavelli, Niccolò, 8, 9, 11, 12, 54
McLachlin (Canadian judge), 32
McLean, John, 102, 112
Madison, James: Berns on, 82n. 34; on blacks, 102; citizenship concept of, 64; colleagues of, 81n. 5; on Constitution, 79; on cultural diversity, 71; on factionalism, 5, 65, 76; on human nature, 65–66, 68, 75; on language, 79, 84n. 53; on limited government, 74; nullification controversy and, 78, 83n. 49; political associations and, 12; on proposed national university, 67; on republican idealism, 7; Scottish Enlightenment and, 11
Maine, 104
male aristocrats, 5
male whites, 57, 80, 113
Mallary, Rollin C., 105
Marshall, John, 106
Marshall, Thurgood, xiv, 101–2, 103, 114, 117nn. 4, 14
Marxists, 10
Maryland, 48
Massachusetts: black citizens of, 118n. 33; educational ambitions of, 58; imprisoned citizens of, 108; independence debate in, 45–47, 48, 52; Pittsfield declaration on, 51
Massachusetts Constitution, 53–54
Massachusetts General Court, 45, 52, 57, 58, 108

Meissner, Doris, 98
men, 5, 57, 80, 113
Mexicans, 89–90
microstates, 5
Middle Colonies, 45
Militia Act (1792), 57
militia service, 57, 113
minority groups, 71, 93, 94. *See also* alien residents; immigrants
Mississippi Supreme Court, 118–19n. 35
Missouri, 11n. 38, 108–9
Missouri Compromise, 104–6, 116–17n. 2, 118n. 31, 120n. 52
Missouri General Assembly, 105
Missouri Supreme Court, 109
monarchy, 35, 51, 52, 69
Montesquieu, Charles Secondat, Baron de, 3–4, 11, 65, 75
Moore, Glover, 105
morality. *See* civic virtue
Morgan, Edmund, 74
Moses (O.T. character), 69
Moynihan, Daniel Patrick, 38
multiculturalism, xi, xii, xiv, xv, 71; Australian, 86; common thread in, 64; denunciation of, 93; particularistic cultures and, 39; professional communities and, 22; progression towards, 88; public schools and, 87. *See also* ethnicity
multilingualism, 40n. 5
multinationalism, 22, 24, 27, 36

Naess, Arne, 15–16n. 6
Natick (Mass.), 52
National Archives, 48
National Commission on Social Studies in the Schools, 93–94
national culture, 3, 71, 87
national identity, 64; deliberation and, 77–78; fluidity of, 78–79; immigrants and, 87; popular virtue and, 66; Publius on, 73–74

universities, 67, 91, 97
unselfishness. *See* altruism
U.S. Bureau of Immigration and Naturalization, 90
U.S. Civil War, 23, 47, 51, 108
U.S. Congress, cynical views of, 8; Immigration and Naturalization Service and, 98; Indians and, 104; militia statute of, 113; Missouri Compromise and, 104–6, 120n. 52; national university proposals and, 67; naturalization and, 103; opening sessions of, 88–89; qualifications for, 118n. 21; restraints upon, 76; welfare restrictions and, 97. *See also* Continental Congress
U.S. Constitution, abolitionism and, 115; age/residency requirements of, 56, 118n. 21; American nationhood and, 47, 71; Berns on, 82 n.34; black commitment to, 115–16; comity clause of, 107, 108; Connecticut oath on, 21, 31; on diversity jurisdiction, 109; Euro-American minority and, 94; Federalist/Anti-Federalist views of, 69; Framers of (*See* Founding Fathers); Hamilton on, 75; immigrants and, xiii, 87; instrumental role of, xii; language of, 78, 96; Madison on, 66, 79; T. Marshall on, 101–2, 103; physical preservation of, 48; protections of, 105, 106, 114, 120n. 53; Publius defense of, 68, 73; ratification of, 112–13, 118n. 33; on slavery, 111–12; state bar membership and, 29; state citizenship and, 110; violation of, 83n. 49; Wiecek on, 117n. 13. *See also* Bill of Rights; Fourteenth Amendment
U.S. Constitutional Convention, 4, 5, 54, 106
U.S. Declaration of Independence. *See* Declaration of Independence

U.S. government. *See* federal government
U.S. Immigration and Naturalization Service, 87, 98
U.S. National Archives, 48
U.S. presidents, 67, 88, 104, 118n. 21
U.S. Supreme Court, 17, 37, 108, 116–17n. 2; *Ambach v. Norwich*, 33; *Cherokee Nation v Georgia*, 104; *Dred Scott v Sandford*, 102, 103, 109–10; *Graham v Richardson*, 96; *In re* Griffiths, 18, 29–31, 32–33

Venetian republic, 2, 5
Vermont, 58
Vesey, Denmark, 107
Virginia, 48
Virginia Constitution, 51–52, 53, 59n. 8
virtue. *See* altruism; civic virtue
voting. *See* elections; franchise
Voting Rights Act, 95

Walzer, Michael, xv, 20, 40n. 8, 63
war, 6
Washington, George, 55, 58, 67, 119n. 41
Washington Legal Foundation, 117n. 4
Wayne, James M., 103
Webster, Noah, 68
welfare benefits, 30, 96, 97
Western Europe, 36, 39
Western India, 90
Western U.S., 89
Whig Party, 88, 112
white persons, alleged superiority of, 110–11, 117n. 13; citizenship of, 114; favoring of, 91; immigration by, 89, 94, 104; male, 57, 80, 113
Wiecek, William M., 117n. 13
Will, George, 65
Williamsburg (Va.), 53

Williams College, 58
Wilson, James Q., 66, 68
Wilsonism, 38
Wisconsin territory, 109
Wolin, Sheldon, 65
women, 55, 56, 113, 117n. 13

Wood, Gordon, 65
World War I, 90, 98
World War II, 90, 91

Yale Law School, 29
Yugoslavia, 47

About the Contributors

Robert A. Dahl, Sterling Professor of Political Science Emeritus at Yale University, is a past president of the American Political Science Association. Among his many books are *Democracy and Its Critics, Dilemmas of Pluralist Democracy: Autonomy vs. Control,* and *Who Governs? Democracy and Power in an American City.*

Susan Dunn is Professor of French Literature and the History of Ideas at Williams College. She is the author of *Nerval et le roman historique* and *The Deaths of Louis XVI: Regicide and the French Political Imagination.* She writes frequently on French and American politics for *Partisan Review.*

Nathan Glazer is Professor of Education and Sociology, Emeritus, at Harvard University. He is the coeditor of the journal, *The Public Interest.* Among his many books are *The Public Interest,* coauthored with Daniel P. Moynihan, *The Limits of Social Policy, Affirmative Discrimination and Ethnic Dilemmas.*

Gary Jeffrey Jacobsohn is Woodrow Wilson Professor of Government at Williams College. He is the author of *Pragmatism, Statesmanship, and the Supreme Court, The Supreme Court and the Decline of Constitutional Aspiration,* and *Apple of Gold: Constitutionalism in Israel and the United States.*

Randall Kennedy is Professor of Law at Harvard University. He is the editor of *Reconstruction.* Among his many writings are *Race, Law, and Criminal Justice,* "Racial Critiques of Legal Education," and "Persuasion and Distrust."

Sanford Levinson is the W. St. John Garwood and W. St. John Garwood, Jr. Regents Chair in Law at the University of Texas Law School. He is the author of *Constitutional Amendment,* and, with Paul Brest, *Processes of Constitutional Decisionmaking.*

Pauline Maier is William R. Kenan, Jr. Professor of American History at MIT. She has written *From Resistance to Revolution: Colonial Radicals and the Development of American Opposition to Britain, 1765–1776,* and *The Old Revolutionaries: Political Lives in the Age of Samuel Adams.*

Noah Pickus teaches at Middlebury College. He is working on a new book, *"True Faith and Allegiance:" Immigration and the Politics of Citizenship.*